Members of the Working Party on Smoking and the Young

Margaret Turner-Warwick DBE DM PhD PRCP President

Stewart W Clarke MD FRCP (Chairman) *Consultant Physician, Royal Free Hospital, London*

Ashley A Woodcock MD FRCP (Honorary Secretary) *Consultant Respiratory Physician, Wythenshawe Hospital, Manchester*

Beulah R Bewley MD FRCP FFPHM *Senior Lecturer in Public Health Medicine, St George's Hospital Medical School, London*

John C Catford DM FRCP FFPHM *Professor of Health Promotion, University of Wales College of Medicine, Cardiff*

Kevin S Channer MD MRCP(UK) *Consultant Physician and Cardiologist, Royal Hallamshire Hospital, Sheffield*

Anne Charlton PhD *Director, CRC Education and Child Studies Research Group, University of Manchester*

Jonathan M Couriel FRCP *Consultant in Paediatrics and Paediatric Respiratory Medicine, Booth Hall Children's Hospital, Manchester*

Jane Dunmore *Director, Parents against Tobacco*

Pamela A Gillies PhD *Senior Lecturer in Public Health, University of Nottingham*

Ann D McNeill PhD *Programme Manager, Smoking Education, Health Education Authority*

P John Rees MD FRCP *Consultant Physician and Senior Lecturer in Medicine, Guy's Hospital, London*

Donald J Reid MA *Director, Programmes Management Division, Health Education Authority*

David Simpson OBE HonMFPHM *Director, International Agency on Tobacco and Health*

Sarah L Stewart-Brown PhD MRCP(UK) MFPHM *Consultant in Public Health Medicine, Worcester and District Health Authority*

John O Warner MD FRCP *Professor of Child Health, University of Southampton*

Jane EM Watkeys MFPHM *Director of Community Child Health Services, Bloomsbury and Islington Health Authority*

Observer

Felicity AH Harvey MB DCM (*Department of Health*)

In attendance

Bernard Lloyd FCCA (*College Secretary*)

Elaine M Stephenson BA (*Working Party Secretary*)

Acknowledgements

The working party is grateful to the following who gave evidence:

Nicholas J Wald FRCP FFPHM (*Professor of Environmental and Preventive Medicine, St Bartholomew's Hospital Medical College, London*)

Martin Jarvis MPhil (*Senior Lecturer, Addiction Research Unit, Institute of Psychiatry, London*)

Joy Townsend MSc (*MRC Epidemiology and Medical Care Unit, Northwick Park Hospital, Middlesex*)

Foreword

The first report on the influences of smoking on health produced by the Royal College of Physicians in 1962 was a turning point in identifying the hazards of tobacco. Specific recommendations were made in subsequent reports which, had they been applied fully, would undoubtedly have already saved the lives of many thousand British smokers. Perhaps more importantly they would have prevented whole cohorts of teenagers in the 1970s and 1980s taking up an expensive and dangerous lifelong habit. This report should spark the new approach required to meet the Government targets on reduction in smoking prevalence. All of us have a responsibility for the health of our children today and in the future.

MARGARET TURNER-WARWICK DBE
President
The Royal College of Physicians
June 1992

Preface

This report is the fifth produced by the Royal College of Physicians on the influence of smoking on health. The previous reports, published in 1962, 1971, 1977 and 1983[1-4] concentrated on the health effects of active smoking and made specific recommendations to try to reduce levels of tobacco consumption. Over the past 30 years, some progress has been made. For example, individual tobacco consumption has fallen and so have deaths from lung cancer in men. On the other hand, lung cancer has continued to rise in women and the uptake of smoking by teenagers has not changed in the last decade. The figure of 110,000 premature deaths resulting from smoking continues to be cited as the burden which society carries.

This report concerns smoking and the young, since new smokers are enrolled almost entirely from this group. Tobacco smoking is addictive and does far greater harm than any other addictive drug. Thus, once children and young people start to smoke, stopping or 'quitting' becomes extremely difficult and the likelihood is that they will continue to smoke into and throughout adult life. Although previous reports recommended a ban on tobacco advertising and promotion, tobacco advertising continues, aided and abetted by voluntary agreements between the tobacco companies and the UK government. Tobacco companies claim not to promote cigarettes to children, but in order to maintain the number of customers they have to replace the 300 smokers who die every day in the UK as a result of smoking. Most new recruits to smoking are under 18 years of age. Much advertising is now subtle and indirect, centering around sporting events such as motor racing with which youngsters identify. Paradoxically, smoking by sportsmen or women would result in a degree of unfitness incompatible with excellence in their chosen sport.

More recently, information has become available on the hazards of passive smoking in the broadest sense. Unwittingly, non-smoking children and adults are placed at risk from others' smoke, as is the unborn child during pregnancy. A report summarising the present evidence, *Passive smoking: a health hazard*, has recently been published (1991).[5]

The facts set out above supplied the rationale of the working party who prepared the report to help protect the future health of young people. The report comes at a time of high government awareness of the role of preventive medicine as set out in its consultative document *The health of the nation*.[6] Many of the responses to this document identified tobacco as the single most important cause of preventable ill-health in the United Kingdom today. The document states the government's intention to reduce the numbers of people starting to smoke and to increase the numbers who stop smoking. The document establishes targets for a national reduction in smoking prevalence by one-third for men and women by the year 2000. Much of this reduction will have to be by prevention of smoking in the young, although this is best achieved in the context of overall reduction in smoking prevalence at all ages. On current trends, it is difficult to see how these targets are going to be met and a new approach is therefore required.

The working party who prepared this report included physicians with an interest in the chest and heart (prime systems damaged by smoking), and experts from child health, public health, epidemiology and health promotion.

The report has been divided into several sections. First, the effects of passive smoking on the health of the fetus and children are described. The health effects of active smoking in children, including aspects of nicotine addiction are considered next, followed by a report on the current prevalence and social factors which come into play. Finally, the working party has produced a series of intervention strategies which are based on the premise that children and young people have the right not to be exposed to the adverse health effects of tobacco, either through passive or active smoking. This places responsibility on all of us and the report proposes how this can be achieved at the level of the family, the school, the media, health service, local and central government.

We hope that the recommendations of this report will be implemented in full so that children in the 1990s will avoid taking up and continuing this expensive and dangerous life-long habit as adults into the 21st century.

The references to this Preface and Chapters 1–6 are given at the end of this Report.

Contents*

*Some of the section headings in this contents list are shortened versions of the headings
that appear in the text.

1 Passive smoking and the health of the fetus

FACTS

1. Babies born to mothers who smoke are lighter by an average 200 grams (approximately half a pound). Paternal smoking also makes babies significantly lighter.

2. Spontaneous abortions (miscarriages) of viable fetuses are increased in pregnant smokers by more than one-quarter (approximately equivalent to 4,300 miscarriages per year in England and Wales).

3. Premature labour is twice as common in pregnant smokers.

4. Perinatal mortality (stillbirths and early neonatal deaths) is increased by approximately one-third in babies of smokers. This is equivalent to approximately 420 deaths per year in England and Wales.

5. The effects of smoking in pregnancy extend well beyond infancy with a reduction in growth and educational achievement.

Introduction

Since the first report in 1957 of the adverse effects of smoking during pregnancy[1] it has been established beyond reasonable doubt that maternal smoking in pregnancy has a significantly adverse effect on fetal growth and the outcome of pregnancy. This, in turn, increases the chances of death and disease in the offspring of smokers.

At the present time, approximately one-third of pregnant women in the UK smoke.[2] Women who smoke in pregnancy are more likely to be younger, single, of lower educational achievement and in un-skilled occupations.[3–5] The male partner is more likely to smoke.[2,5] Only one in four women who smoke succeed in stopping at some time during pregnancy. Women who succeed in giving up are more likely to be from professional and managerial families.[2] Surveys have found that between one-fifth and one-third of women recall receiving advice about smoking during pregnancy.[2,5–7]

Unfortunately, almost two-thirds of women who succeed in

stopping smoking in pregnancy restart again after the birth of their baby.[8]

Smoking reduces birth weight

Low birth weight, irrespective of the cause, is bad for babies. It is associated with higher risks of death and disease in infancy and early childhood. Low weight for the length of pregnancy is described as inappropriately small for gestational age (SGA) and is the result of intrauterine growth retardation (IUGR).

Infants born to smoking mothers are of lower birth weight,[9] with a mean reduction in birth weight of 200 grams (approximately half a pound) compared with those born to non-smoking mothers.[10,11] Smoking increases the risk of having an SGA infant as much as three-fold.[12] The effect is more pronounced in older mothers, with a mean reduction of 301 g and a five-fold increase of IUGR in women under 35 years, whilst the figures are 134 g and two-fold respectively in women under 17 years. The effect may also be additive with other environmental effects on the fetus, such as alcohol, that result in lower birth weight. In one study there was a mean reduction in birth weight of 500 g in mothers who smoked and drank heavily as compared to those who neither smoked nor drank.[13]

The effect is dose-related, with higher smoking rates (10–20 cigarettes per day) leading to a greater shortfall in birth weight.[14] More sophisticated studies that measured serum cotinine (the principal metabolite of nicotine) to indicate the amount of smoke inhaled have demonstrated a dose-response effect (see also Chapter 2). A group of women with the highest levels of serum cotinine had babies with birth weight 441 g less than those with the lowest levels.[15] A reduction of birth weight of 12 g for every cigarette smoked per day, or 25 g for every microgram of urine cotinine per mg creatinine has also been demonstrated.[16] There are now several reports (eg Refs 17–19) which confirm the finding from a large retrospective study[20] that the effect of smoking in pregnancy is due mainly to smoking in the second and third trimesters (Fig. 1.1).

It has been suggested that some of the association between cigarette smoking in pregnancy and low birth weight might be spurious since a number of other socio-demographic variables associated with smoking are also likely to be associated with low birth weight.[21] However, there is now incontrovertible evidence to confirm an independent association of smoking with low birth weight. The dose relationship already described is strong evidence of causal association, particularly as the effect is most closely associated not with the

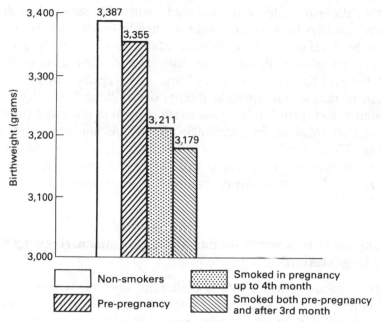

Fig. 1.1 *Effect of maternal smoking on birthweight. Comparison of non-smokers, pre-pregnancy smokers and those who were smoking after the third month. [20]*

number of cigarettes smoked but with the amount of smoke inhaled.[15] The fact that the effect of smoking is largely confined to the second and third trimesters is strong evidence of a direct influence on fetal development since the other socio-economic factors do not alter during pregnancy. Several studies have used multivariate analysis to account for other variables including maternal age, weight and height; weight gain during pregnancy; number of previous pregnancies; socio-economic status; race and sex of offspring.[1,14,22–26] However, far from being a dependent variable, there is evidence that smoking has the greatest effect on birth weight and also that the effects of other variables such as social and psychological factors are largely mediated through their association with smoking.[25] It has been suggested that the relatively low perinatal mortality in mainland China is due to a low incidence of low birth weight babies and that this in turn is partly due to low rates of smoking by pregnant women.[27]

Other adverse effects of maternal smoking on fetal growth

The lower birth weight of infants of mothers who smoke is associated with shorter length and smaller head circumference.[28] However, weight is the parameter most affected, with the result that SGA infants of smokers have lower weight for height index than the whole group of SGA infants.[29] As with SGA infants as a whole, the growth deficit persists into childhood[29,30] so that children of smoking mothers are smaller and lighter at five years[29] and seven years;[31] this effect is also seen in normal birth weight infants of smokers.[29] Smaller head circumference at birth implies poor brain growth *in utero* and there is evidence that smoking in pregnancy affects the intelligence of the offspring. Thus, a follow-up of the 1958 national cohort at the age of 23 years showed a strong correlation between smoke exposure in pregnancy and lower academic attainment even after allowing for social class.[32]

Smoking increases spontaneous abortion (miscarriage up to 28 weeks gestation)

The spontaneous abortion rate is higher in smoking women.[20,33,34] This holds true even when other variables are taken into account with an overall 27% higher abortion rate.[35] Whilst most abortuses are chromosomally abnormal or have gross congenital malformations, abortuses of women who smoke are more likely to be chromosomally normal. However, the effect on pregnant women who smoke over the age of 30 may be different, with an increase in chromosome abnormalities in this age group.[36] Thus, for young mothers, smoking increases their chances of losing a potentially normal offspring, and for older mothers, smoking increases the chances of abnormalities in the offspring. This increase is equivalent to approximately 4,300 smoking related miscarriages per year in England and Wales (see Appendix 1).

Smoking increases perinatal mortality (from 28 weeks gestation up to 7 days of life)

Placenta praevia (displaced placenta)[37] and placental abruption (early separation)[37,38] are significantly more common in women who smoke and may be among the reasons for the observed increase of poor fetal growth and, more importantly, preterm delivery (early delivery of less mature baby). Preterm delivery is more common among smokers, possibly as much as two-fold,[39] and is even more apparent in older women.[40] It is responsible for part of the excess morbidity and mortality[20,37,41,42] and is greater in mothers who smoke in the latter half of pregnancy (see Fig. 1.2).[20] The increased perinatal mortality in smoking mothers occurs particularly among

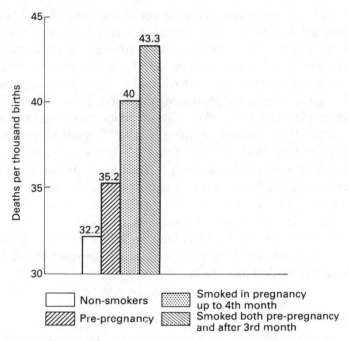

Fig. 1.2 *Effect of maternal smoking on perinatal mortality. Comparisons of non-smokers, pre-pregnancy smokers and those who were smoking after the third month. [20]*

manual socio-economic groups and in groups that are already at high risk of perinatal death, such as older mothers or those who have had a previous perinatal death.[43] The association with perinatal death is stronger if maternal smoking is assessed objectively by the measurement of serum cotinine rather than the reported number of cigarettes smoked.[44] The excess perinatal deaths attributable to maternal smoking is approximately 420 per year in England and Wales (see Appendix 1).

Mechanisms

Some of the effects of smoking on perinatal mortality may be mediated through the effects of smoking on birth weight. This arises both by an increase in preterm delivery and by IUGR affecting the infant's weight more than its length or head circumference. This particular subgroup of SGA babies, with a low weight for height index, into which infants of smoking mothers fall, carry the highest morbidity and mortality of the SGA group as a whole.[45] Excess morbidity and mortality in babies of smoking mothers is therefore caused not just by low birth weight but by other factors which also affect health and survival. The frequency of acidosis[39] and low abnormal Apgar scores (a measure of well-being of the newborn infant based on vital signs) at 1 and 5 minutes after birth is greater in infants whose mothers have smoked in pregnancy.[46] A large number of potentially important effects on the placenta and fetus are seen in smokers which may provide clues to the pathophysiology of both low birth weight and increased mortality. These effects include reductions in placental blood flow, fetal activity and breathing movements;[47] histological changes in the placenta;[48] reduced prostacyclin synthesis in the umbilical artery;[49] abnormal levels and ratios of trace elements such as cadmium and zinc;[50] changed relationships between maternal plasma constituents such as cholesterol and carotene;[51] subtle changes in fetal DNA which are in turn associated with low birth weight.[52] The US Committee to Study the Prevention of Low Birth Weight noted that the effects of smoking on infant birth weight do not seem to have changed over the past two decades in spite of substantial reductions in the tar and nicotine content of cigarettes.[53]

Illness in childhood

We have already referred to the continuing effects of smoking in pregnancy on growth in childhood but it becomes increasingly difficult to separate the effects of prenatal exposure from those of postnatal exposure to smoke in the home environment (passive smoking) beyond the immediate perinatal period. This makes it difficult to interpret a number of studies that show increased morbidity in infants and children born to mothers who smoked in pregnancy. Clearly, from the child's perspective, it is immaterial whether the prenatal or postnatal exposure is the more important but, to save repetition, most concerns about morbidity in childhood are dealt with in the chapter on passive smoking (Chapter 2).

Maternal smoking has been associated with elevated cord blood IgE levels and with a five-fold higher incidence of subsequent atopic symptoms in the infants. This latter finding was especially prominent for infants born to non-atopic parents.[54,55] Infants of mothers who smoked in pregnancy had significantly more hospital admissions with respiratory illnesses in the first year of life even within subgroups defined by birth weight, birth order and socio-economic status.[56] Clearly, these observations were confounded by the effects of postnatal exposure to passive smoking. However, one study using prospective data found that maternal smoking in pregnancy influenced the incidence of respiratory illnesses in children rather more than passive postnatal smoking.[57]

Several studies have highlighted an effect of maternal smoking on lung function in children, but the influence of ante- and postnatal smoking was not separated.[58,59] There is a clear link between maternal smoking and Sudden Infant Death Syndrome (SIDS)[60] (see also Chapter 2) but the mechanism requires further elucidation. The earlier age of death in SIDS infants of mothers who smoke compared with those who do not suggests that an antenatal influence may be important.[61] An association has been reported recently between smoking in pregnancy and childhood cancers,[62] although earlier studies found the association to be weak.[63]

Paternal smoking reduces birth weight

The effect of paternal smoking on fetal outcome is rather less well established, but may also be important. Most studies show that it has an effect on birth weight,[64–67] but one failed to confirm the association.[24] One study estimated that, on average, birth weight is reduced by 120 g per pack of cigarettes smoked by the father per day,[66] and in this and another similar study[67] the reduction in birth weight was rather larger than might be expected from the presumably small amount of smoke inhaled passively by the mother as compared with mothers who smoke. It remains to be established whether this effect is due to pregnant mothers' passive smoking or to direct damage to the sperm. The latter has been suggested by the finding of cotinine in seminal fluid of smokers,[68] and is well summarised in a recent letter to the *Lancet*.[69]

Possible interventions

The earlier a woman gives up smoking in pregnancy, the better will be the health of her baby[70] and the greater will be the likelihood that she remains a non-smoker throughout pregnancy and for up to six months after the baby's birth.[71] Ideally, women should give up smoking before conception, but studies suggest that giving up even after the onset of pregnancy might prevent many of the unwanted effects on pregnancy. Such interventions have been carried out[72] and have been shown to be effective in preventing low birth weight.[73] Although informal smoking cessation advice is probably frequently given to pregnant women, few women actually recall it being given.[2,5,7] Formal and effective provision of smoking cessation advice, counselling and support is much less common. Provision of such advice should be universal and demanded by purchasing authorities from provider units under the new Health Service contracts.

Some costs of smoking in pregnancy

It has been estimated that maternal smoking during pregnancy in the USA in 1983 was responsible for about 14.5% of all low-weight births, for 6.6% of all admissions to neonatal intensive care units, and represented about 8.5% of national expenditure on neonatal intensive care services, or $272 million.[74] Excess perinatal care attributable to smoking costs the NHS millions of pounds.

Conclusions

The fetus and the newborn

■ Antenatal passive smoking by the fetus is one of the most important avoidable risk factors for fetal morbidity and death.

Costs: human and fiscal

■ UK data on smoking prevalence in pregnancy are only available for a few areas. This makes it difficult to determine the precise cost. However, the cost in terms of human suffering is high, with thousands of unnecessary miscarriages and hundreds of babies dying unnecessarily in the perinatal period. The increased neonatal morbidity incurs the expenditure of millions of pounds in avoidable neonatal intensive care.

The need for advice and counselling

■ Provision and planning of smoking cessation services during antenatal care is currently inadequate and should be improved. Only a minority of women recall receiving advice from their GP or obstetrician. Midwives have a critical role to play, both at antenatal clinics and in the community.
■ Smoking cessation advice, counselling and support should be offered to all women of child-bearing potential and should be routinely available from trained personnel in all antenatal clinics.

2 Passive smoking and the health of children

FACTS

1. Children of parents who smoke inhale nicotine in amounts equivalent to their actively smoking 60–150 cigarettes per year.

2. Over one-quarter of the risk of death due to the Sudden Infant Death Syndrome (cot death) is attributable to maternal smoking (equivalent to 365 deaths per year in England and Wales).

3. Infants of parents who smoke are twice as likely to suffer from serious respiratory infection.

4. Symptoms of asthma are twice as common in the children of smokers.

5. One-third of cases of 'glue ear', the commonest cause of deafness in children, is attributable to parental smoking.

6. Children of parents who smoke more than 10 cigarettes per day are shorter than children of non-smokers.

7. Passive smoking is an important cause of school absenteeism, accounting for one in seven days lost.

8. Parental smoking is responsible for at least 17,000 admissions to hospital each year of children under the age of five.

9. Passive smoking during childhood predisposes children to developing chronic obstructive airway disease and cancer as adults.

10. Maternal smoking during pregnancy and infancy is one of the most important avoidable risk factors for infant death.

Introduction

In the last decade there has been increasing evidence of the harmful effects on non-smokers of inhaling the cigarette smoke of smokers, so called 'passive' or 'involuntary' smoking.[1,2] Whilst the risks of passive smoking are less than those of active smoking, they are nonetheless significant. For example, non-smoking adults who inhale the cigarette smoke of others for a prolonged period have a risk of developing lung cancer that is 10–30% higher than non-smokers who are not regularly exposed to tobacco smoke.[2]

Children spend much of their early life in the presence of their parents and, if their parents smoke, these children will be exposed for long periods to environmental tobacco smoke (ETS). The respiratory system of the young child is particularly vulnerable because it is structurally and immunologically immature and is developing rapidly. Thus, there has been great interest in the effects of passive smoking on the health of children, with over 120 papers published on the subject since 1980. The important findings of this research are summarised below.

Composition and measurement of environmental tobacco smoke

Tobacco smoke in the environment is derived from two sources:

(i) *Mainstream smoke*   This is the complex aerosol inhaled by the smoker, much of which is deposited in the respiratory tract but some is exhaled;
(ii) *Sidestream smoke*   This arises from the burning tip of a cigarette and accounts for 85% of environmental tobacco smoke.

Both types contain measurable quantities of gaseous and particulate toxins including carbon monoxide, ammonia, formaldehyde, nicotine and hydrogen cyanide, and potent carcinogens including benzo(a)-pyrene, 2-naphthylamine, benzene and dimethylnitrosamine. Many constituents are in higher concentrations in the particulate phase of sidestream smoke than in mainstream smoke. The amount of these chemicals that are inhaled passively depends on the type and number of cigarettes smoked, the proximity of the non-smoker to the smoker and the size and the ventilation of the room.[1,3]

It is difficult to quantify the 'dose' of ETS that passive smokers inhale. Early studies of passive smoking in childhood relied on a history of whether one or both parents smoked, and in some studies, of the number of cigarettes they consumed each day. More recent studies have quantified exposure to ETS by measuring levels of a biochemical marker of tobacco smoke, cotinine. Cotinine, a metabolite of nicotine, is a sensitive (97%) and specific (99%) indicator of smoking. It can be measured in saliva and urine, and has a half-life of 18–24 hours. The salivary cotinine concentration of schoolchildren correlates strongly with the smoking habits of their parents, and particularly with those of their mothers.[4] There is a reasonable degree of stability of these concentrations over a year.[5] Cotinine levels in children correlate closely with air nicotine levels measured within the home and with answers to questionnaires about household smoking.[6] The correlation between the number of smokers in the household and the child's salivary cotinine has been confirmed, but significant levels of salivary cotinine have also been found in schoolchildren from non-smoking households.[7] This indicates the importance of children's exposure to ETS from sources other than their parents. On average, children have higher cotinine levels in the winter than the summer; children from families of manual social classes and those who live in rented accommodation have higher levels than would be predicted from the number of smokers in their households. This suggests that relative overcrowding may be important in determining the extent of exposure. Simply enquiring about parents' smoking habits may lead to an inaccurate assessment of a child's ETS intake. It has been suggested that multiple cotinine measurements are needed to establish a stable profile of exposure to ETS.[8] Although cotinine measurements provide a more objective assessment of recent exposure to ETS, they do not provide information about the duration of exposure or about the intake of other components of ETS, which may be of more clinical importance than nicotine. Nevertheless, from the data on cotinine levels, it has been estimated that the total nicotine dose received by the children of smoking parents is equivalent to their actively smoking between 60 and 150 cigarettes per year.[5]

There are other difficulties in interpreting and comparing studies of passive smoking in children.[1,3,9] Prospective, case-control and cross-sectional study designs have been used. Different, and often poorly defined, outcome measures have been employed. The degree to which other variables which influence child health, and particularly respiratory health, such as socio-economic status, maternal age and education, prematurity and family size, have been controlled for, varies greatly. Because 90% of women who smoke during pregnancy are still smoking five years later,[10] it is difficult to separate the intrauterine effects of maternal smoking from the effects of postnatal passive smoking. Despite these difficulties there is remarkable consistency in the conclusions of studies about the effects on the child of parental smoking.

Maternal smoking increases death in infancy

Several large population studies have examined the relationship between maternal smoking and death in early childhood.[11-13] There has been particular interest in the association between smoking and the sudden infant death syndrome (SIDS), which is defined as the sudden unexpected death of an apparently healthy infant, in whom a thorough post-mortem examination fails to reveal an adequate cause of death. SIDS accounts for 30–48% of deaths between the ages of one week and one year.

In a study of over 305,000 infants born in Missouri, Malloy and others explored the association between maternal smoking and the age and cause of 2,720 infant deaths.[11] The infant mortality rate for all causes was 12.1 deaths per 1,000 live births among infants of smokers compared with 7.6 among infants of non-smokers (odds ratio 1.6).* After adjustment for other variables such as maternal age, education and marital status, and the child's birth weight, smoking was more strongly associated with post-neonatal death than with neonatal death (death within the first 28 days of life). The adjusted odds ratio for smoking was particularly high for deaths from respiratory disease (mean odds ratio 3.4) and SIDS (mean odds ratio 1.9). The authors estimated that if no mother had smoked, then the mortality from all causes would have been reduced by 10%, from SIDS by 28%, and from respiratory illness by 46%. They concluded that respiratory deaths and SIDS may be related to postnatal passive exposure of the infant to cigarette smoke, and not simply to maternal smoking during pregnancy.

Maternal smoking as a risk factor for the Sudden Infant Death Syndrome was examined in a prospective study of 99% of all births in Sweden over a three-year period.[12] There were 190 cases of SIDS amongst 260,000 live births (0.7 per 1,000), representing 27% of all infant deaths between one week and one year of age. Maternal smoking was the single most important preventable risk factor for SIDS. The same study estimated that if maternal smoking could be eliminated, the number of SIDS would be reduced by 27%, an attributable risk remarkably similar to that from the Missouri study.[11] There was a definite dose effect: women who smoked 1–9 cigarettes per day had relative risk of SIDS of 1.8, and those who smoked ten or more a day had a risk of SIDS 2.7 times higher than non-smoking mothers. The increased risk associated with smoking was most evident in infants who died in the first 10 weeks of life. This finding agrees with data from a United Kingdom study of 988 infant deaths, which also showed a dose-related effect of maternal smoking on the incidence of SIDS.[13]

---

*An odds ratio of 1.6 means that the likelihood of the disease or disorder under study is 60% higher in the study group (smoking mothers) than in the control (non-smoking group).

These studies demonstrate that babies born to mothers who have smoked during pregnancy and after giving birth have a significantly higher risk of dying in infancy than infants of non-smoking mothers. After controlling for other factors known to be associated with infant mortality, this risk persists and is related to the mother's daily cigarette consumption. The risk from smoking seems to be greatest for deaths from respiratory disease and SIDS which are the most common causes of death in this age group. It is not clear how maternal smoking predisposes to infant death, nor do the data allow us to separate between the effects of antenatal and postnatal exposure. However, they do show that maternal smoking is a most important preventable risk for death in early childhood. For example, if we apply the Swedish attributable risk estimates to data for England and Wales, where 1,326 deaths were classified as SIDS in 1989,[14] elimination of maternal smoking would result in 365 fewer deaths each year.

Passive smoking increases respiratory illness in childhood

There is convincing evidence that parental smoking increases the risk of respiratory illness in childhood.

Respiratory illness in infancy

In a prospective study of 10,672 infants, Harlap showed a definite dose-response relationship between maternal smoking and hospital admissions for bronchitis and pneumonia.[15] This relationship was most evident in infants 6–9 months of age. A prospective longitudinal study of 2,200 children in Greater London found that the incidence of pneumonia and bronchitis was clearly associated with the parents' smoking habits: if both parents were non-smokers the annual incidence was 7.8%; if one parent smoked it was 11.4%; and if both parents smoked it was 17.6% ($p<0.0005$).[16] As in Harlap's study,[15] the effect of smoking was independent of birth weight, socio-economic class and family size. In a cohort of 1,180 New Zealand children followed from birth, a dose-related effect of maternal smoking on the incidence of pneumonia, bronchitis and bronchiolitis in infancy was shown.[17] In this study, infants of smoking mothers were twice as likely to have a consultation for respiratory illness as infants of non-smokers. Infants admitted to hospital with respiratory syncytial virus bronchiolitis or pneumonia are more likely to have mothers who smoked at the time of admission than matched control subjects.[18]

A recent study of respiratory illness in infancy provides the most

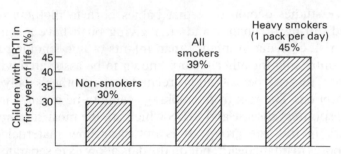

Fig 2.1 *The percentage of children with lower respiratory tract infections (LRTI) in the first year of life in relation to maternal smoking* (From data in Ref 19).

detailed evidence of the risks associated with parental smoking.[19] In this prospective study of 850 infants, the numbers of episodes of wheezing and non-wheezing lower respiratory illness were significantly increased if the mother smoked; the overall odds ratio was 1.52 if the mother smoked, and 1.82 if she smoked more than 20 cigarettes a day (Fig. 2.1). There were no differences between the infants of mothers who smoked both antenatally and postnatally and those who smoked only after birth: the amount smoked was more important than the timing of exposure. Infants of mothers who smoked developed respiratory illnesses earlier than those of non-smokers. Infants who did not attend day-care nursery were at increased risk from maternal smoking, perhaps because they have more prolonged exposure to smoke. In this study, smoking by fathers had no detectable effect.

A retrospective analysis of data from the Child Health and Education Study confirmed these adverse effects of maternal smoking, but suggested that smoking during pregnancy was more important than smoking in the postnatal period.[10] By contrast, a large study from Shanghai, where women do not smoke during pregnancy, found that the admission rate for respiratory illness was correlated with the daily cigarette consumption of family members.[20] The adjusted odds ratio was 1.89 for infants from families who smoked more than 10 cigarettes per day compared to non-smoking families. This study is particularly important because it demonstrates that postnatal passive smoking has a definite influence on respiratory illness that cannot be explained by maternal smoking during pregnancy.

Respiratory illness in the older child

The relationship between parental smoking and respiratory symptoms in children over the age of two is less clear, and several studies that have shown a definite harmful effect in infancy have found no significant effect in older children.[16,21]

Nevertheless, a survey of over 15,000 8–19-year-olds showed a positive correlation between parental smoking and frequent coughs in children who had never smoked.[22] Thirty-five percent of boys under 11 whose parents did not smoke reported frequent coughs; if one parent smoked this increased to 42%, and if both smoked the proportion was 48% ($p<0.0001$). The pattern in girls was similar. Mothers' smoking had more influence than fathers'. In a prospective study of 4,800 5–11-year-olds, there was a significant association between the frequency of wheeze, cough, and episodes of bronchitis, and the number of cigarettes smoked by the parents.[23] For example, the relative risk of having frequent wheeze rose from 1.0 if neither parent smoked to 1.3 if they smoked 10 cigarettes per day, and to 1.6 if they smoked 20 per day. Analysis of data from the Harvard longitudinal study revealed a highly-significant dose-response relationship between maternal cigarette consumption and the frequency of eight defined respiratory illnesses or symptoms in 6–9-year-olds.[24] Current maternal smoking increased the frequency of these illnesses by between 20% and 35%. Paternal smoking had a smaller but significant effect.

Passive smoking and the child with chronic lung disease

The studies described so far have examined the effects of passive smoking in unselected populations of children. It is likely that children with a pre-existing chronic lung disorder may be particularly susceptible to the adverse effects of ETS.

Asthma is the commonest chronic illness of childhood, affecting between 10–15% of children. There is considerable evidence that passive smoking increases the frequency and severity of symptoms in children with asthma. In an analysis of data on 4,000 children aged 0–5 years Weitzman found that maternal smoking of more than 10 cigarettes a day was associated with higher rates of asthma (odds ratio 2.1), an increased likelihood of using asthma medication (odds ratio 4.6), and an earlier onset of asthma (odds ratio 2.6) than was observed in the children of non-smoking mothers (Fig. 2.2).[25] Hospital admissions for acute asthma were not significantly increased by maternal smoking. In a prospective study of 9,670 British children followed from birth, 18% of children had recurrent wheeze by the age of ten.[26] The incidence of recurrent wheeze was increased by 14% when mothers smoked over four cigarettes a day, and by 49% when mothers smoked 15 or more a day. Gortmacker analysed data from 4,000 children and found

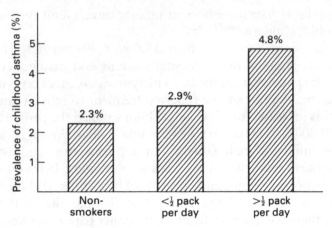

Fig 2.2 *Prevalence of childhood asthma in relation to maternal smoking status* (From data in Ref 25).

that maternal smoking increased both the prevalence and severity of asthma.[27] The attributable risk associated with maternal smoking was estimated to be between 18–34% in this population. After controlling for other variables, the presence of one or more smokers in the household of asthmatic children increased by 63% the number of visits to the emergency room, but not the admissions to hospital for the treatment of asthma.[28]

Studies of passive smoking in children with asthma have shown that maternal, but not paternal, smoking increases the frequency and severity of asthma symptoms. When compared with asthmatic children whose mothers did not smoke, the children of smoking mothers had lung function indices that were 13–23% lower, and a four-fold greater degree of responsiveness to histamine challenge, indicating abnormal airway narrowing and bronchial hyperreactivity.[29] Boys, and children with atopic dermatitis, were particularly susceptible to the adverse effects of maternal smoking, which increased with the duration of exposure to ETS, the age of the child, and the season of the year.[30–32] Several studies of the determinants of the onset of childhood asthma have found maternal smoking to be an important factor,[33] but others have found no such association.[8,21]

Passive smoking affects other childhood chronic respiratory diseases. Rubin demonstrated a dose-dependent effect of parental smoking on the severity of disease, hospital admission rate, weight and height in children with cystic fibrosis.[34] Passive smoking is an important predisposing factor for respiratory syncytial virus infection in children with bronchopulmonary dysplasia, a chronic lung disease of preterm infants who have required mechanical ventilation.[35]

Passive smoking adversely affects lung function

The effects of passive smoking on lung function in children and adolescents have been assessed in over 15 studies: these are reviewed in greater detail elsewhere.[1,7,36] The results of these studies differ, at least in part because of differences in the populations studied and in study design.[9] Some studies have found a significant association between parental smoking and lung function, but others have not. Overall, data from both cross-sectional and longitudinal studies have shown a dose-related reduction in lung function. Maternal smoking appears to be more important than paternal smoking. Younger children appear to be more adversely affected than older children. Whether passive smoking has a direct toxic effect on the lung, or an indirect influence by increasing the child's susceptibility to infection or to the development of atopy is unknown.

Some of the most convincing evidence that passive smoking has a significant and deleterious effect on lung function has come from the Harvard longitudinal study of childhood risk factors for the development of adult chronic obstructive airway disease (COAD).[24,36,37] In a 7-year prospective study of 1,156 children and adolescents from this cohort,[37] there was a significant association between maternal smoking and a lower forced expiratory volume in 1 second (FEV_1) and forced mid-expiratory flow rate. Maternal smoking significantly lowered the expected increase in FEV_1 by 7–10% over this period, even after correction for confounding influences.

Few of the studies of passive smoking and lung function have used objective measures of exposure to ETS. However, Strachan, in a recent cross-sectional survey of 770 7-year-old Scottish schoolchildren, showed that spirometric indices of airway function were inversely related to salivary cotinine levels, in a pattern suggesting damage to the small airways.[7] The differences in lung function indices between those children with the lowest cotinine levels and those in the top quintile were small (approximately 7%). In this study, and another from the Harvard cohort,[38] there was no evidence that passive smoking increased non-specific bronchial hyperreactivity. However, Martinez showed that parental smoking did increase bronchial hyperreactivity.[39,40] These apparently conflicting results are likely to reflect differences in the methods of assessing bronchial hyperreactivity used in the different studies.

Overall, the data from these studies suggest that prolonged passive smoking in childhood results in a reduction in lung size of between 1% and 5%, an effect that is unlikely to produce a detectable health consequence in childhood.[1,3] However, this reduction may be of relevance to the development of chronic obstructive airway disease in adult life. It is important to note that the best predictor of who is likely to develop COAD is the level of pulmonary function in early adult life.[3]

Ear, nose and throat problems are increased by passive smoking

Persistent middle ear effusion (secretory otitis media, 'glue ear') is the commonest cause of deafness in children. It may result in delayed language development, and educational and behavioural problems.[41] Up to 80% of children will develop a middle ear effusion by the age of five, and 10–20% will have had such an effusion in the previous year. Persistent middle ear effusion is the commonest cause for children to need an operation, and 5–10% of all children will have ENT surgery for this condition.[42]

Many factors influence the development of middle ear effusion (MEE), and there have been several studies of the relationship between parental smoking and MEE.[41–44] Kraemer compared 76 children with persistent MEE and significant hearing impairment, who were admitted for the insertion of grommets, with a matched control group. The presence of more than one adult smoker in the household was associated with a significantly higher risk of developing MEE. There was a complex interaction between passive smoking, MEE and a history of nasal congestion or atopy in the child.[43] In a detailed case control study of the aetiology of glue ear, Black showed that parental smoking significantly increased the risk of undergoing surgery for glue ear in 150 children aged between four and nine (mean relative risk 1.64).[44] In a study of 700 7-year-old schoolchildren, Strachan assessed the contribution of passive smoking to the development of MEE.[42] The overall prevalence of middle ear effusion, as measured by impedance tympanometry, was 9.4%. There was a highly significant trend for more abnormal tympanograms with higher salivary cotinine levels. The authors estimated that at least one third of MEE in this age group may have been attributable to passive smoking. Iverson found that parental smoking was the only home environmental factor that influenced the prevalence of MEE.[45] He estimated that parental smoking accounted for 15% of MEE in children aged 1–7, and 36% of MEE in 6–7 year olds.

Many cases of MEE follow acute otitis media. More than 70% of children will have had at least one, and a third will have had more than three, episodes of otitis media by the age of three. Parental smoking increases the risk of single and recurrent episodes of acute otitis media.[46]

The mechanism by which passive smoking causes middle ear disease is unclear. ETS may have a direct effect on the mucosa of the middle ear resulting in oedema, abnormal mucociliary clearance, blockage of the eustachian tube, and impaired ventilation of the middle ear. There may be an indirect effect by adenoidal enlargement, or by increasing the number of infections.

Parental smoking also affects the noses and throats of children. A significant association has been found between the frequency of sore throats in children and maternal smoking.[47] Corbo showed a clear dose-effect relationship between habitual snoring in children and parental cigarette consumption, suggesting that passive smoking has a chronic effect on the upper airways of children.[48] Said showed a significant relationship between the number of cigarettes smoked by the parents and a history of adenoidectomy and tonsillectomy.[49] Children who had two parents who smoked were almost twice as likely as the children of non-smokers to have had such surgery. As most children have adenotonsillectomy because of recurrent or persistent ear or upper airway symptoms, Said concluded that passive smoking increases the frequency or severity of these symptoms.

Parental smoking affects children's growth

Infants born to mothers who have smoked during pregnancy are lighter and shorter than infants of non-smoking mothers (see Chapter 1). There have been studies of the effects of passive smoking on postnatal growth. Berkey analysed the height and the height growth rate of 9,273 American schoolchildren and assessed the association between passive smoking and growth between the ages of 6–11 years.[50] Children of mothers who smoke were shorter than those of non-smoking mothers ($p<0.001$). There was a strong negative correlation between the attained height and the number of cigarettes that the mother smoked each day. The authors made no correction for the parents' heights, the level of smoking during pregnancy, or the birth weight of the child. The differences in height were small: if the mother smoked ten or more cigarettes a day, then the mean height of her child was 0.65 cm less than that of a non-smoking mother. Paternal smoking had no significant effect. Because there were no differences in the rate of growth between the two groups, the authors concluded that the difference in attained height was the result of exposure to cigarette smoke in early childhood or *in utero*.

Data on 5,903 primary school children who had been enrolled at birth into the British National Study of Health and Growth were analysed by Rona *et al.*[51] They tested the hypothesis that passive smoking may have an effect on a child's growth separate from that due to the mother's smoking during pregnancy. The height of the child was significantly associated with the number of cigarettes smoked by the parents, even after allowing for the parents' heights, the child's birth weight, maternal smoking during pregnancy and other factors. The number of cigarettes smoked at home was more strongly related to the height than the number smoked by the mother in pregnancy. Fathers' smoking had a definite effect on the child's attained height. Children whose parents smoked more than ten cigarettes a day were on average 0.6 cm shorter than those of non-smoking parents.

These studies show that children of parents who smoke are on average 0.5–1.0 cm shorter than children of non-smokers. Whether the effect of passive smoking on height is indirect, for example by altering eating habits, or by increasing respiratory infections in early childhood, or whether it has a direct toxic effect, is not known. Whilst the possible mechanisms are of interest, the magnitude of the effect is of little clinical significance.

Other effects of passive smoking

Parental smoking increases hospital admissions

Three studies have documented an increase in hospital admissions amongst the children of mothers who smoke. Harlap examined admissions of infants in Jerusalem in the 1960s and calculated a relative risk of 1.2 amongst the children of mothers who smoked during pregnancy, when compared to non-smoking mothers.[15] Another study in Finland recorded a relative risk of 1.35 for hospital admissions amongst 0–5-year-olds whose mothers had smoked during pregnancy.[52] There was a similar relative risk for British 0–5-year-olds who were enrolled into the 1970 birth cohort study.[53] This study differs from the other two in that the risks were examined in relation to the mother's smoking habits when the child was five years of age, and not simply during pregnancy. The risks were adjusted to take into account confounding social and family variables. This study showed there was a dose-response relationship between the number of cigarettes smoked by the mother and the risk of hospital admission—(mean relative risk 1.1 for 1–9 cigarettes a day, 1.2 for 10–19 cigarettes a day, and 1.3 if more than 20 cigarettes were smoked by the mother each day).

The relative risks calculated from these studies are too large to be accounted for by admissions to hospital for lower respiratory tract disease or middle ear effusion, the two specific conditions for which a definite effect of passive smoking has been shown. This suggests that passive smoking increases the risk for other conditions in childhood. Using the relative risks from the 1970 birth cohort study, it is possible to estimate that in England and Wales a minimum of 17,000 children under the age of five were admitted as a result of their mothers' smoking (Appendix 2).

Increased school absenteeism in the children of smokers

Charlton and Blair studied the impact of parental smoking on school absenteeism amongst 2,800 12–13-year-old children in the north of England.[54] Maternal smoking was associated with an increased rate of absence from school. This effect persisted even after adjustment for the children's own smoking habits, and the school catchment area. From the results of this study it is possible to calculate that 13.5% of school absenteeism in this age group can be attributed to the effects of passive smoking (Appendix 3).

House fires

Smokers' materials are the most frequent cause of fatal house fires, accounting for 39% of all deaths due to ignition in 1990 (Home Office Fire Statistics). Between 70 and 95 children in the United Kingdom die each year in house fires, and many more are seriously and permanently injured.

Adult diseases

Evidence is now emerging that prolonged passive smoking during childhood may be important in the development of 'adult' diseases, such as coronary artery disease[55] and cancer.[56] As recurrent respiratory illness and abnormal lung function in childhood are important factors in the development of adult chronic obstructive airway disease, passive smoking in childhood may prove to be an important contributory factor to that disorder.[2,57] As will be discussed in later chapters, the smoking habits of parents are an important influence on whether their children will become active smokers in adolescence.

Conclusions

■ It is clear that passive smoking imposes a significant, and potentially avoidable, burden on the health of children.

Effect on early life

■ The excessive respiratory morbidity associated with passive smoking is most evident and most serious in the first two years of life, when the respiratory system of the young infant is structurally and immunologically immature.

Childhood disease caused by passive smoking

■ The mother's smoking habits are more important than the father's. The children of smokers are more likely to be admitted to hospital, more likely to suffer from bronchitis, pneumonia and bronchiolitis, and more likely to have recurrent wheeze or persistent cough than the children of non-smokers. Parental smoking increases the frequency and severity of the symptoms of asthma. Passive smoking in childhood results in small but significant changes in lung function that indicate abnormal function of the small airways. Exposure to environmental tobacco smoke (ETS) is an important factor in the aetiology of recurrent ear, nose and throat problems in children, particularly with persistent middle ear effusion; the latter is the commonest cause of deafness and the commonest reason for surgery in childhood. As would be expected from a pollutant that increases the risk of respiratory infection, ETS is an important cause of school absenteeism. A causal relationship between passive smoking and all of these diseases is supported by the consistency of the different studies, the dose-response relationship, and the biological plausibility.

Effect of avoidance

■ Avoidance of exposure to ETS offers an opportunity to reduce respiratory morbidity in children. Unlike many other effects of non-smoking in which the health benefit is relatively long term, the effect of avoiding passive smoking would be noticeable almost immediately in reduced numbers of GP consultations for childhood respiratory infections, lower referral rates from hearing screening programmes, less need for operations for glue ear and reduced rates of school absenteeism.

▓ Maternal smoking during pregnancy and infancy is the most important avoidable risk factor for infant death. Elimination of maternal
smoking during this critical period could result in a substantial
reduction in mortality, particularly from the sudden infant death
syndrome and respiratory disease.

Education and advice

▓ We can no longer afford to be complacent about the hazards
of passive smoking. Environmental tobacco smoke is the most
common and the most important indoor pollutant. It contains
carcinogens and other toxic chemicals which are inhaled by children
and enter their bloodstream. All of those responsible for the health of
children should inform parents of the risks to their children through
smoking in the home. Pregnant women, who are already warned
about the possible effects of smoking on the fetus, need to know that
their children are at risk from parental smoking after birth, and
should be offered support and guidance to give up smoking.[57]

3 Active smoking and the health effects for children

FACTS

1. Nicotine is a drug of addiction. Many young smokers are addicted to nicotine and develop withdrawal symptoms on stopping.

2. Smoking is an important marker for other types of drug abuse, eg alcohol, cannabis, cocaine etc.

3. Young smokers have more respiratory infections with more time off work and school.

4. Teenage smokers have 2–6 times more cough and sputum than non-smokers.

5. Asthmatics who smoke have worse symptoms and lung function than non-smoking asthmatics.

6. The earlier children start smoking, the greater the risk of lung cancer.

7. Smoking is a cardiac stimulant, which magnifies the effect of stress on the heart.

8. Smokers are less fit as is shown by their being slower both at sprints and endurance running. The performance in a half marathon of a smoker of 20 cigarettes per day is that of a non-smoker 12 years older.

9. Smoking increases blood coagulability and adversely affects blood lipids.

10. Subarachnoid brain haemorrhage is six times more common in young smokers than non-smokers.

11. The earlier children start smoking, the younger they develop heart disease.

12. Smoking increases skin ageing and wrinkling.

13. Female smokers are 2–3 times more likely to be infertile.

14. Smoking affects immunity and has been associated with an increased risk of acquiring HIV-1 infection.

Introduction

The effects of passive smoking in childhood have been shown in Chapters 1 and 2. However the effects of active smoking are considerably greater and most smokers begin the habit while they are under the age of sixteen. Coronary artery disease, lung cancer, chronic bronchitis and emphysema make up the most common serious complications of cigarette smoking. They are rarely seen as clinical problems before middle age. However, there is evidence that the problems begin soon after smoking is taken up and that the effects are increased by the length and intensity of exposure.

Nicotine as a drug of addiction

Mechanism and effect of addiction

Regular tobacco use is a form of drug addiction mediated through behavioural and pharmacological effects of nicotine.[1] Smoking is a form of systemic drug administration which delivers nicotine directly into the pulmonary circulation rather than the systemic or portal circulations. Nicotine reaches the brain about 10 seconds after inhalation, twice as fast as when given intravenously.[2] Smokers can manipulate the dose of nicotine on a puff-by-puff basis.[3]

Tobacco deprivation in smokers produces a syndrome of irritability, lack of concentration, cognitive impairment and weight gain which can be partially relieved by oral nicotine gum. However one symptom, the desire to smoke, is not reliably diminished by nicotine gum and there may be two reasons for this. First, the speed of delivery of a drug can affect the reinforcing efficacy (eg the inhaled form of cocaine, crack, is more reinforcing and dependence-producing than other forms of cocaine).[4] Second, stimuli associated with a method of drug taking (eg taste and smell) may be important.[5]

The pattern of smoking is influenced by the pharmacodynamics of nicotine. Nicotine has a half-life of two hours and continues to accumulate for 6–8 hours after the commencement of regular smoking. The first cigarette produces a substantial pharmacological effect, but at the same time acute tolerance begins to build. With a succession of cigarettes, nicotine accumulates in the body, resulting in a greater degree of tolerance and subsequently, as nicotine levels fall, more intense withdrawal symptoms. Nicotine is almost totally eliminated from the body overnight allowing partial re-sensitisation to its action. The duration of time between cigarettes through the day may be determined as a time at which there is some regression of tolerance (so that the nicotine has a substantial acute effect) but before severe withdrawal symptoms occur.[2]

The likelihood of progression from occasional to addictive tobacco use is considerably higher for tobacco than for other addictive drugs.[1] After initiation, the smoker gradually increases to a stable level of consumption; only 10% of regular adult smokers smoke less than five cigarettes per day. Approximately four out of five smokers would like to stop and two in every three smokers have made at least one serious attempt to do so.[1,6]

Addiction in the young

The inhalation of cigarette smoke by young people leads to an early pharmacological dependence on cigarettes and many children underestimate the addictive nature of smoking. Saliva cotinine concentrations in 11–16 year old smokers have been measured to examine the extent of tobacco smoke inhalation. Cotinine concentrations among young regular daily smokers indicated that they were already inhaling substantial doses of nicotine which were likely to be having some pharmacological effects. Comparisons with adult smokers suggested that they were inhaling a similar dose of nicotine per cigarette. This means that from a very early stage nicotine can play an active role reinforcing smoking.[7,8]

The majority of these young smokers reported subjective effects of smoking (ie smoking gave them a 'buzz'), that they had made attempts to stop, and that they suffered withdrawal symptoms during abstinence which were related to self-reports of cigarette consumption, depth of inhalation and measures of nicotine intake.[9,10] In one study, in spite of being counselled about their smoking behaviour, 97% of the daily smokers were still smoking two years later.[8] These findings point to an early development of dependence on cigarettes.

Cigarette smoking and other drug abuse

The health risks for young smokers go beyond the impact of smoking itself as their smoking forms just one part of a lifestyle which contains multiple health risks. Alcohol consumption is related to smoking: 49% of 11–15-year-old regular smokers have a drink at least once a week, compared to only 6% of non-smokers from the same age-group. Experimentation with illegal drugs is widespread amongst older smokers. Only 2% of 11–15-year-old non-smokers have ever tried drugs such as cannabis, LSD, heroin, cocaine or crack; this compares with 18% of occasional smokers and 50% of regular smokers of the same age.[11] It has long been considered that smoking is a precursor or gateway drug but the evidence for this is still unclear;[12] nevertheless, it is important as a marker of risk for other drug abuse.

Respiratory disease is increased in young smokers

The symptoms associated with chronic respiratory disease become more common within a year or two of taking up smoking. Many studies of teenagers have shown that this is true for the common respiratory symptoms: cough, sputum production and shortness of breath. The results of studies of lung function have not been so clear although significant abnormalities have been found in young smokers. It is perhaps not surprising that the lung function results are less clear than the evidence on symptoms. Although most chronic heavy smokers develop respiratory symptoms, only a minority will develop significant problems with chronic airflow obstruction.

Asthma

In asthma the airways show increased responsiveness, reacting adversely to numerous provoking factors such as inhaled irritants. Both passive[13] and active smoking are capable of producing problems in asthma.

Among teenagers, smoking increases problems from asthma[14] and the respiratory function abnormalities associated with smoking are more marked in asthmatics.[15] One study of 11–16-year-olds showed that asthma was more common among children who smoked[16] but that the onset of the asthma symptoms preceded the start of smoking. It is unlikely that asthmatics are more inclined to take up smoking; a more likely explanation is that smoking increases the chances that asthma symptoms will persist.

An Australian study of asthma,[17] starting with children below the age of 7 years, has shown that by the age of 21 years the progress of asthma is less satisfactory in smokers. The number of cigarettes smoked in the intervening period and the current consumption are both related to poor asthma control.

Respiratory tract infections

Investigations of rates of respiratory tract infections in smoking and non-smoking children have produced variable results. Where recall of previous events is relied on, rates have been increased slightly or not at all[18,19] but studies which recorded events prospectively are likely to be more reliable and these have shown infections to be more common in young smokers.

A study in Sydney, Australia using annual questionnaires found more episodes of acute bronchitis in smoking children, especially in girls.[15] In 94 student nurses, half of whom were smokers, respiratory tract infections were more common and lasted longer in smokers, leading to an average extra 2–3 days absence over a year.[20] In 2,885 12–13-year-olds followed for four months, minor ailments and time off school were greater in smokers.[21] An early study of 14–19-year-olds at boarding school used infirmary records to show that all types of respiratory illness were greater in smokers[22] and this was most evident for severe lower respiratory tract infections. However, not all studies are consistent. Kujala's study of over 1,000 20-year-old conscripts, which found a five-fold increase in cough and a decline in lung function, showed no evidence of increased respiratory infections in the records of smokers.[23]

Overall, reliably recorded retrospective and prospective studies do show higher rates of respiratory infections in young smokers leading to more time off school and work. A reduction in smoking would produce a substantial fall in general practitioner workload, since respiratory tract infections form a major part of the family doctor's practice.

Cough, sputum and shortness of breath

There are a large number of studies in the young which compare common respiratory symptoms between smokers and non-smokers. Most of the work is in teenagers but information on the direct effect of smoking is available down to the age of ten years. All the studies show that smoking increases symptoms even at this age when length of exposure has been short. Wheezing is a characteristic feature of asthma but seems to have a wider distribution related to other symptoms such as cough and sputum production and with a positive association with smoking.

In the 10–12-year age group, two studies in the 1970s from Bewley *et al.*[24,25] showed a doubling of the prevalence of respiratory symptoms amongst those who smoked even though their definition of smoker was just one cigarette or more weekly. One of these studies[24] separated an urban-rural effect on symptoms but the effects of cigarette smoking were independent of the excess in respiratory symptoms related to living in an urban area.

Various reports provide information on more than 50,000 subjects in the 10–20-year age range. Five large studies contribute 40,000 subjects.[19,24,26–28] Nearly every report has been able to demonstrate in-

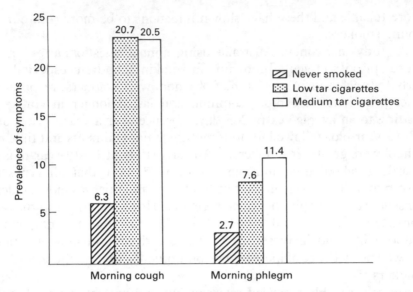

Fig. 3.1 *Prevalence of respiratory symptoms in 16–18 year olds according to smoking habits* (Adapted from: Rimpela AH, Rimpela MK, *Br Med J* 1985; **290**: 1461).

creases in the rates of cough, sputum, wheeze and shortness of breath, usually an increase between two and six times the non-smoking rate (Fig. 3.1). The definitions used for smokers have varied from more than one cigarette per week to more than 9 cigarettes per day. Other factors are associated with respiratory symptoms throughout childhood but by the age of 20 years the most important cause of such symptoms is smoking.[26]

Most studies have looked at the amount smoked and the length of smoking history but few have detailed the type of cigarette smoked. However, in one study of 5,000 16–18-year-olds[28] symptoms were increased to a similar extent by low or middle tar cigarettes.

The prevalence of symptoms does increase with the amount smoked both in terms of the number of cigarettes smoked each day and the length of the smoking history.[26,29] However, even small numbers of cigarettes smoked regularly produce symptoms in fairly short times; certainly one year is long enough to create problems.[15,30]

Little information is available on the effects of stopping smoking on symptoms in this age group. Since gross changes in lung function have not occurred, on stopping smoking one would expect a major reduction in the symptom of breathlessness over time. Cough and sputum production in adults decline on stopping, and this would seem to be even more likely in children and adolescents where smoke exposure has been less. Most studies which include young ex-smokers find their symptom levels to be intermediate between smokers and non-smokers.[15,18,19]

Lung function

Each inhalation of cigarette smoke provides a temporary broncho-constriction, usually mild and lasting less than a minute in smokers and non-smokers at all ages.[31] In some subjects more prolonged airway narrowing occurs on smoking and with time lung damage may become irreversible.

Many different tests of lung function have been performed in the assessment of smoking effects in the young. Broadly, they can be divided into conventional spirometric measures of FEV_1 and FVC* or more sophisticated tests designed to look at early evidence of disease, particularly those related to the small airways of the lung. These have included maximum expired flows at low lung volumes and tests of abnormalities of distribution on ventilation such as closing volume. Most of these investigations have shown abnormal lung function associated with smoking in 12–20-year-olds, which is probably present by the age of 14 years in smokers. The interpretation of tests of lung function is complicated by the growth expected in teenage children. However, the consistency of the findings indicates the strength of the relationship between smoking and lung function.

As with respiratory symptoms, definitions of smoking in lung func-tion studies have varied from more than one cigarette per week to more than ten per day. There is again evidence of a dose effect based on the number of cigarettes smoked each day.[32,33] Differences in starting levels of lung function in young smokers and non-smokers may be related to differences in maturity and to social factors determining who takes up smoking, eg the more mature children in a given age group may be more likely to smoke. One study[34] has found that children who take up smoking seem to start with higher baseline levels of lung function but that five years of smoking bring their lung function levels down to that of the non-smoking group. Other estimates are that smoking from the age of 15 years will lead to a reduction of FEV_1 by the age of 20 to 92% of the expected level, and a reduction of FEF25-75 to just 90% of the predicted value.[14] A recent study[35] followed a group of 15–40-year-olds over 8 years. The effect of smoking on FEV_1 decline was again dose related. Overall one pack per day led to a drop of 8.4 ml per year, 65 ml over the 8-year study. In addition, smoking which had taken place before the study seemed to have a slight continuing effect over the 8 years.

*FEV_1 (forced expiratory volume in one second) is a measure of airway function. FVC (forced vital capacity) measures the total volume exhaled from the lungs.

Only 20–25% of smokers eventually develop serious problems with airflow obstruction from chronic bronchitis and emphysema. The physiological changes found in young smokers might be just a marker of cigarette smoking or the beginning of a more serious decline in function which will continue for a minority as long as they continue to smoke. Many of the studies in children have been cross-sectional studies which show differences between smoking and non-smoking groups but are limited by the lack of knowledge of starting levels and progression. One small study[34] found abnormalities in airflow at low lung volumes in 20% of young smokers. Corin *et al.*[37] followed up a small group of smokers, ex-smokers and non-smokers over four years and found progression of lung function abnormalities in the smokers. This applied to flow at low lung volumes, increased compliance, increased total lung capacity and residual volume but not FEV_1 and flow at 50% of vital capacity (V_{max50}). Other larger longitudinal studies have shown decline in FEV_1.[35]

The single breath nitrogen test is an assessment of the evenness of gas distribution in the lung. Evidence from adults suggests that most of those subjects who will show a rapid decline in FEV_1 in relation to their smoking have abnormalities in the single breath nitrogen test when FEV_1 is still normal.[38] However, abnormalities in the single breath test were often found in those whose FEV_1 did not decline excessively fast over the next 10 years so that this test is not sufficiently specific to act as an early warning of future problems. Studies of susceptibility to lung function changes[39,40] have suggested that respiratory symptoms are markers for a faster decline in lung function. This has not been consistent in all studies[35] and these interrelationships are difficult. Symptoms may indicate an underlying susceptibility or may be induced by smoking in parallel with lung function decline. Personal smoking and symptoms have a greater effect than parental smoking.[39]

In general, the tests of lung function can be divided into sophisticated tests of gas distribution and simpler tests which reflect lung volumes and airway narrowing. There is evidence from cross-sectional reports over a wide range from teens to sixties that abnormalities in tests of gas distribution (such as closing capacity and the slopes of Phase 3 of the alveolar washout) do not progress much with age[41] and may return to normal on stopping smoking.[42] In contrast, the indicators of airway narrowing and lung volume, such as FEV_1, FVC and V_{max50}, become progressively abnormal with length of smoking history, starting from teenage years[35,39,41,43,44] and do not return to normal on stopping smoking. Therefore, changes found solely in gas distribution tests can be reversible markers of the smoking habit, whereas decline in FEV_1 or FVC indicates permanent lung damage which begins soon after children begin to smoke.

Other respiratory abnormalities

Early studies of alveolar lavage using fibreoptic bronchoscopy found marked changes in the lavage fluid from smokers.[45] This technique washes cells from the alveoli and the small airways of the lungs. More cells, mainly macrophages and neutrophils, come from the lungs of smokers and show subtle changes. These cells are probably recruited as part of the body's defence against the inhalation of cigarette smoke and it is likely that some of the cells may be related to the development of lung damage. These cellular changes in the lavage fluid are found in young asymptomatic smokers.

Smoking for more than one year results in a decrease in the muco-ciliary clearance of the lungs,[46] the mechanism by which the small airways clear themselves of secretions and inhaled particles. Niewoehner et al.[47] examined lung histology in 20 non-smokers and 19 smokers who had died suddenly outside hospital at an average age of 25 years. The smokers all showed evidence of inflammatory changes in their small airways while such changes were rare in non-smokers. These morphological changes show the early effects of cigarette smoke related damage and probably correspond to the minor lung function changes which are seen in young smokers. No data are available on histological damage in even younger groups of smokers.

Lung cancer is the commonest malignant cause of death in most developed countries and cigarette smoking accounts for most of this mortality. Such cancers are rare under the age of 30 years but smoking in childhood provides the potential for future trouble. The risk of lung cancer is related to the length of time of smoking and not just to the total exposure, so 20 cigarettes per day for 30 years produces a greater risk than 40 cigarettes daily for 15 years.[48] Those who start before the age of 20 are at considerably greater risk than those who start later.

Adverse cardiovascular effects in young smokers

Acute physical effects of smoking cigarettes

Smoking a cigarette causes immediate effects on the body. Heart rate increases within one minute of starting smoking and may increase by up to 30% in the first 10 minutes. Peripheral vasoconstriction and changes in regional blood flow occur and as a consequence blood pressure also increases acutely by 7–10%.[49] Abstinence from regular smoking for 24 hours causes a reduction in resting heart rate of about 10 beats per minute but the first cigarette smoked after this period causes an immediate increase.[50] After the first cigarette no further increase in

heart rate occurs with subsequent smoking which suggests that physiological tolerance has developed. The change in heart rate is directly
related to the amount of nicotine in the cigarette.[51] Thus, it seems likely
that the changes in heart rate and blood pressure are caused by the
effects of nicotine absorbed from cigarette smoke which is known to
cause stimulation and then paralysis of the autonomic ganglia. Carbon
monoxide in cigarette smoke may also be responsible for some of these
effects.

In parallel with the increase in heart rate that occurs following
smoking, changes in intracardiac conduction have been found. An
electrophysiological study showed that atrio-ventricular conduction
time was significantly shortened by cigarette smoking, but intra-atrial,
intra-ventricular and His bundle-Purkinje conduction times were
unaltered.[52] These changes reflect the sympathomimetic effect of inhaled nicotine. Changes in intracardiac conduction may provide
arrhythmias even in people without heart disease, but a large study of fit
American policemen[53] showed no difference in ventricular ectopic
counts precipitated by exercise in smokers and non-smokers. However,
in patients with acute myocardial infarction, smoking was associated
with increased frequency of ectopic beats.[54] In patients with chronic
stable angina or a previous history of myocardial infarction smoking
was actually associated with a fall in ectopic frequency—but
most patients in this study were taking drugs with anti-arrhythmic
properties.[55]

Smoking increases the physical effects of stress on the body and does
not, as commonly supposed, cause the smoker to relax. Studies using
video games as psychological stressors have shown that this stress causes
an increase in heart rate of about 12 beats per minute and in systolic
blood pressure of about 15 mmHg in males and 7 beats per minute and 5
mmHg in females. Smoking during these activities causes a further
increase in these parameters with an increase in heart rate for both sexes
of about 30 beats per minute and systolic blood pressure of about 20
mmHg.[56] The pattern of cardiovascular response differs between the
sexes: in young women, smoking causes an increase in heart rate and
diastolic blood pressure but in men the increase is greater for systolic
blood pressure. This is not explained simply by differences in body
size.[57] Other factors may influence the cardiovascular response. In a
study comparing physical stress in young women, using the cold
pressor test where a hand is immersed in a bucket of iced water (5°C) for
1 minute, with mental stress, using a mental arithmetic test under time
pressure for 1.5 minutes, smokers who were concomitantly taking the
oral contraceptive pill had exaggerated responses to mental but not
physical stress[58] compared with smokers who were not taking the oral

contraceptive pill. In the long term, the body adapts to the adrenergic effect of smoking by down regulation of β-adrenergic receptors. In a study of monozygotic twins discordant for smoking habit over 20 years, the density of β-adrenergic receptors on lymphocytes was 40% lower, although the total circulating plasma catecholamine levels were higher in smokers by nearly 75%.[59]

Smoking and physical fitness

Smokers are less fit than non-smokers. In a large study of young army recruits, smokers were twice as likely to fail to complete basic training compared with non-smokers.[60] In studies of endurance exercise, smokers reach exhaustion earlier than non-smokers and derive less benefit from training.[61] In one study of 6,500 19-year-old army conscripts, smokers ran a significantly shorter distance in 12 minutes compared with non-smokers, and the more cigarettes smoked per day and the longer the duration of smoking the shorter the distance run

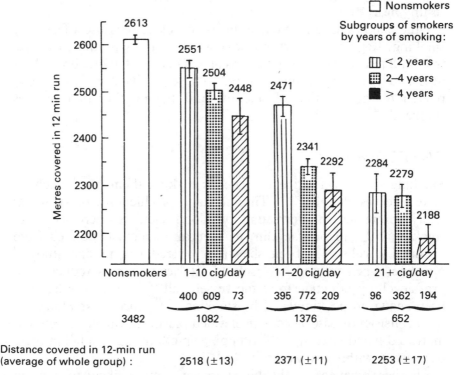

Fig. 3.2 *Performance in 12-min run among 6,592 Swiss 19-year-old military conscripts according to number of cigarettes smoked and years of smoking* (From: Marti B, Abelin T, Minder C, *Prev Med* 1988; **17**: 79).

(Fig. 3.2). The same non-smoking recruits ran an 80 metre sprint in a significantly shorter time than smokers.[62] In the same study, of 4,100 regular joggers who took part in a yearly 16 km race, smokers were consistently slower. It was estimated that for every cigarette smoked per day the time to complete the run was increased by 40 seconds. The authors suggested that smoking 20 cigarettes a day increased the time taken to run the 16 km by the equivalent of 12 age-years or destroys the endurance enhancing effect of running 20 km per week.[62]

How does smoking cause these effects? Regular smokers have an increased amount of carboxyhaemoglobin in their blood, thus reducing its oxygen carrying capacity and shifting the oxyhaemoglobin dissociation curve to the left. Klausen *et al.*[63] showed that smoking three cigarettes before exercise reduced the duration of exercise by 20%, but inhaling carbon monoxide before exercise in doses equivalent to those obtained from smoking decreased exercise duration only by 10%. Thus, the effects of smoking are not all explained by the increase in carboxyhaemoglobin. Chronic sympathetic stimulation caused by smoking increases resting heart rate and basal metabolic rate and offsets the advantages of endurance training which causes a reduction of resting heart rate.

Other studies have shown that short-term exercise is also affected by smoking. Regular smokers are twice as likely to discontinue exercise treadmill tests because of symptoms of exhaustion, fatigue, breathlessness, and leg pain than non-smokers.[64] These disadvantages are directly related to the duration of smoking and the number of cigarettes smoked.[62–65]

Clotting factors

Smoking causes activation of platelets making them more likely to adhere to vessel walls.[66–68] Thromboxane production from platelets which promotes the formation of blood clots is increased after smoking[69–71] and prostacyclin, its natural antagonist, derived from endothelial cells, has been shown to be reduced in one study.[72] Nicotine, when infused into isolated arteries, causes a reduction in prostacyclin production from the vessel wall.[73] Fibrinolysis has also been shown to be stimulated by smoking.[74,75] Chronic smoking has been consistently associated with elevated plasma fibrinogen levels and increased blood viscosity.[76–80] Stopping smoking causes a fall in these parameters within two weeks.[81–83]

All these changes in the blood make it more likely to clot; in consequence, smoking is strongly associated with occlusive vascular disease affecting the coronary, cerebral and peripheral arteries.

Blood lipids

Smoking also has adverse effects on blood lipids. Following a fatty meal serum triglycerides are significantly higher in smokers than non-smokers and HDL cholesterol (which has a beneficial effect) lower.[84] A recent overview[85] of all the published data on smoking and lipids showed that on average smoking increases blood cholesterol by 3.0%, triglycerides by 9.1% and lowers HDL cholesterol by 5.7%. There is evidence for a dose-response curve, so that the more cigarettes smoked the greater the changes in the lipids. Moreover, when cigarette smoking is given up, the lipid profile returns quickly towards normal, certainly within 30 days.

Many epidemiological studies have shown a clear-cut relationship between total blood cholesterol and the risk of developing coronary artery disease. It has been estimated that for every 1% increase in total cholesterol the risk of death from coronary artery disease increases by 2%.[86] It has also been shown that high levels of HDL cholesterol are associated with a lower risk of coronary heart disease. Since smoking causes an increase in total cholesterol but a fall in HDL cholesterol these changes clearly increase the risk of coronary artery disease.

Pathogenesis of vascular disease in smokers

The degenerative process by which arteries thicken and narrow by the deposition of lipid rich deposits (atherosclerosis) increases with age. These deposits occur particularly at sites where arteries branch and cause gradual narrowing of the lumen but remain below the endothelium. If the endothelium splits over the site of an atheromatous deposit, the underlying lipid is exposed to the circulating blood and attracts platelets. Once platelets adhere to the vessel wall a thrombus quickly forms which comprises strands of fibrin and cells. The artery is rapidly occluded, cutting off the blood flow to the organ it is supplying. Should this happen in a coronary artery, myocardial ischaemia results and eventually tissue necrosis and infarction. About 90% of myocardial infarctions are caused by a thrombus blocking an artery, often at the site of an atheromatous deposit.[87] However, in 70% of cases the deposit is not large and by itself would not cause a severe stenosis. Thus, dissolution of the clot by activating the fibrinolytic mechanism by drugs can be markedly effective in improving prognosis following an infarct.[88] Similarly, drugs which make platelets less sticky and therefore less likely to adhere to the vessel wall also reduce coronary events.[89] By comparison, smoking promotes clotting in the blood and thereby increases the risk of heart attacks.

Heart disease

Myocardial infarction is not just a problem for the elderly and can occur in people less than 40 years old. When it does so, all published studies have shown a very strong link with smoking cigarettes.[90–94] In all studies smoking was the dominant risk factor occurring in 66–90% of subjects with other risk factors like hypertension (11–33%) and hyper-cholesterolaemia (21–49%) occurring in far fewer patients. In smokers with coronary artery disease, quitting reduces mortality and complications within twelve months and is further evidence for the pathogenic effect of smoking.[95–97]

Stroke

When a cerebral artery is occluded by thrombus, permanent damage occurs resulting in a stroke usually causing weakness of one side of the body. Ischaemic stroke in young people (less than 45 years of age) has also been shown to be associated with smoking, with at least a doubling of the risk.[98,99] Stopping smoking reduces this risk by the end of two years and by the end of five years the risk is the same as in non-smokers.[100]

Subarachnoid haemorrhage from ruptured cerebral aneurysms has been shown to occur up to six times more frequently in smokers[101–103] compared with non-smokers. There is also an interaction in women between smoking and the use of oral contraceptives so that the two factors combined increase the likelihood of subarachnoid haemorrhage by up to 22 times.[102,104]

Peripheral vascular disease

Narrowing of the arteries in the legs reduces blood flow to the exercising muscles and causes pain in the legs on walking (claudication). If the narrowing progresses gangrene of the foot and toes can occur. This form of arterial disease occurs virtually exclusively in smokers (>90%)[105] with a nine-fold increase in risk of claudication in smokers of more than 15 cigarettes per day. Arterial reconstruction surgery using veins to bypass blockages can be effective but continued smoking causes the grafts to block sooner.[106,107] Three-year survival in patients with peripheral vascular disease is significantly reduced in heavy smokers (>15 cigarettes a day) compared with moderate smokers (<15 cigarettes a day) with a 10-fold increase in the need for amputation.[108] Thromboangiitis obliterans (Buerger's disease)[109] is a rare form of peripheral vessel arteritis which is almost entirely confined to young men between the ages of 20 and 40 years who are heavy cigarette smokers. The disease is more common in Israel, Japan and India and certain genetic predispositions have been identified by blood group typing (HLA-A9; HLA-B5). The peripheral arteries and veins in the limbs are inflamed and damaged resulting in blockage by thrombus formation leading to tissue ischaemia often with ulcer development. The association with smoking is so strong that abstinence can lead to resolution of the lesions. However, if patients continue to smoke, amputation is inevitable.

Overall cardiovascular health risk

Smoking cigarettes has been shown to be the major cause of coronary artery disease and it has been estimated to be responsible for 43–70% of the deaths (US Surgeon General) from coronary artery disease.[110,111]

Other adverse effects of smoking in young people

Smoking is associated with a large number of medical problems. Apart from bronchogenic carcinoma, tumours of the larynx, pharynx, mouth, oesophagus, pancreas, kidney and bladder are more common in smokers.

Oral lesions such as leukoplakia and depigmented lip patches are more common in young smokers.[112] Smoking produces premature facial wrinkling.[113] Female smokers are two to three times more likely to be infertile.[114] Fitness levels are lower and exercise tolerance is reduced in young people who smoke.

Smoking alters immunity.[115] Recent data suggest that smokers are more likely to become infected by HIV (even after other risk-taking behaviours have been accounted for)[116] and HIV-positive smokers progress to AIDS more quickly than HIV-positive non-smokers.[117]

Conclusions

Addiction

▪ Many childhood smokers are pharmacologically dependent on cigarettes (ie are addicted) and stopping smoking is associated with withdrawal symptoms. Smoking in children is associated with other forms of drug abuse, including alcohol.

Dangers to health

■ Diseases in many body systems are associated with cigarette smoking. Most of these conditions appear in adulthood and many of them are related to a cumulative risk from cigarette smoking. It would be expected that smoking, whenever it begins, will contribute to the risk. Since the length of smoking exposure is an important factor, those who start smoking in childhood strikingly increase the risk of future problems.

Respiratory disease

■ It is remarkable that abnormalities in respiratory symptoms and in lung function can be detected so early on and with such comparatively light exposure. This shows clearly the potency of the damaging agent. Children who smoke have evidence of current disease as well as a store of problems for the future if they continue to smoke.

■ Reductions in respiratory infections which would follow a reduction in smoking would have a major immediate impact on general practitioner workload. The earlier that children start smoking the greater the risk of lung cancer.

Cardiovascular disease

■ Smoking cigarettes has an immediate stimulating effect on the cardiovascular system which is associated with a reduction in cardiorespiratory fitness. The main effects on health, however, occur later in life, and the earlier children start smoking the greater the risk of occlusive arterial disease causing stroke, myocardial infarction and peripheral vascular disease. These diseases remain the largest cause of mortality in the United Kingdom.

Premature ageing and infertility

■ Active smoking has a variety of other adverse effects on the health of young people, including premature facial wrinkling, infertility and susceptibility to HIV infection and AIDS.

4 Prevalence and development of smoking in young people

FACTS

1. In Great Britain 450 children start smoking every day.

2. One-quarter of UK school leavers aged 15 years smoke regularly, ie at a time when it is illegal to sell them cigarettes. Little change has occurred in the last decade. Present data suggest more girls than boys now smoke.

3. By the age of 11 years one-third of children, and by 16 years two-thirds of children have experimented with smoking.

4. Most adult smokers started regular smoking before the age of 18 years.

5. The high prevalence of regular smoking in young people and the lack of any significant decline in the last decade is alarming.

Prevalence of smoking

Prevalence in the UK

Since 1982, national surveys have been carried out by the Office of Population Censuses and Surveys to determine the prevalence of smoking (ie the proportion of the cohort that are current smokers) among secondary school pupils aged 11 to 16 years.[1] Smoking varies from region to region[1,2] and also varies between schools within regions.[1-3] The five completed national surveys up to 1990 showed little change in the prevalence of regular smoking since 1982, with as many boys as girls smoking in England (Fig. 4.1). A similar pattern has been observed in Scotland and Wales. In Wales, however, in 1990, significantly more girls overall (11%) than boys (8%) were regular smokers in the 11–16-year age range,[1] and this is also now true for young adult females. There are approximately 650,000 children in each annual cohort in Great Britain, and statistics of onset indicate that approximately 450 children start smoking every day. Regular smoking in children is defined as being at least one cigarette per week.[4]

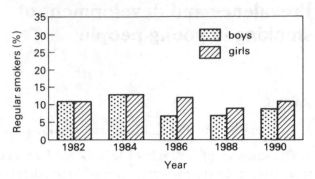

Fig. 4.1 *Regular smoking by sex in children 11–16 years, England 1982–90. [1]*

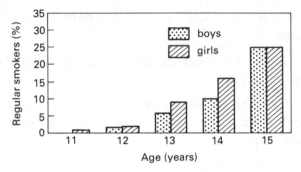

Fig. 4.2 *Regular smoking by age and sex, England 1990. [1]*

The prevalence of smoking in school-leavers is high. In 1990, 25% of both girls and boys in the sample from England were smoking regularly in year eleven, ie aged 15–16 years.[1] The prevalence of regular smoking increases steadily with increasing age (Fig. 4.2). The greatest increase takes place between the ages of 14 and 15 years in both boys and girls. General Household Survey statistics show that, up to the present time, after school leaving age, whilst in the 16 to 19 year age group young men's smoking prevalence continues to equal that of young women, in the 20–24 year age group more females than males now smoke.[5]

At the age of 16 years, proportionally more non-smokers stay at school and enter the sixth form than leave school for vocational colleges, employment or unemployment.[6] Smoking prevalence in 16-year-olds at further education colleges has also been shown to vary widely according to the vocational subject they study. For example, 50% of hairdressers, 44% of pre-nursing students and 20% of catering and engineering students have been found to be regular smokers.[7]

Prevalence in Europe and around the world

As Table 4.1 shows, with the exception of Israel which has a low level of smoking in teenagers, in the majority of developed countries around the world, approximately one in five of 15-year-olds smoke at least weekly. Although the *incidence* of smoking (uptake of smoking or new cases) in young people is generally falling, the *prevalence* is still high enough in young women and men to give rise to considerable cause for concern. In industrialised countries prevalence studies of tobacco use show that by the end of adolescence, at about 18 years of age, most of those destined to become daily smokers later in life are already smokers and are at risk of future health problems (see Chapter 3).

Most of the prevalence data on smoking presented here have been collected using self-completed questionnaires. The validity of self-reported data on smoking has been challenged on the grounds that young people are likely either to under-report because they perceive it to be socially unacceptable to indulge in the habit or, alternatively, over-report to boast. Evidence does however exist to suggest that adolescents do provide accurate self-reports of their smoking. Of samples of saliva taken from young people to assess levels of cotinine present (metabolite of nicotine), only 1% did not match self-reported smoking.[8]

Level of consumption of cigarettes in young people

Equal proportions of girls and boys now smoke at the secondary school age level, but girls generally smoke fewer cigarettes than boys. The median number of cigarettes smoked by regular smokers in the week before the 1990 National Survey was 48 for boys and 40 for girls, which is a substantial increase in consumption since 1982 for both boys and girls (from 40 and 36 respectively).

The consumption of two packets of cigarettes on a weekly basis is sufficient potential for a serious health problem.[9] Once smoking at this level, it is not easy for young people to give up the habit.

Experimentation with smoking

The younger a person becomes a regular smoker the greater the risk to their health and the earlier the onset of lung cancer[10] and heart disease[11] in later life. It is therefore important to consider prevalence, and patterns of experimentation and initiation of smoking in young people.

Table 4.1 Data on smoking prevalence of 15-year-olds, drawn from: (a) Six recent national studies, and (b) The WHO Cross-National Study of Children's Health Behaviour, 1986. Figures are in percentages

Country	Smoke daily	Smoke weekly	Smoke once per week or more	Smoke less than weekly	Do not smoke (have tried)	Have never smoked	Number in sample
All countries							
M	14.4	4.4	22.3	6.4	39.9	34.2	>5,754
F	14.4	5.6	28.0	8.0	36.3	36.3	>5,934
Australia							
M	—	—	25.0	—	—	—	—
F	—	—	28.0	—	—	—	—
Austria							
M	11.8	6.5	—	10.3	43.3	28.2	476
F	13.1	7.1	—	11.8	39.1	28.9	381
Belgium							
M	16.6	5.0	—	5.1	32.7	40.6	603
F	13.5	6.2	—	5.6	29.4	45.3	502
Canada*							
M	17.4	—	—	—	—	—	—
F	17.8	—	—	—	—	—	—
Finland							
M	29.1	6.3	—	6.3	39.9	18.4	539
F	20.1	7.4	—	10.1	36.8	25.6	543
Hungary							
M	20.4	5.9	—	8.2	39.9	25.4	562
F	14.1	6.8	—	8.2	42.2	28.7	704
Israel							
M	5.7	3.5	—	3.5	30.9	56.4	402
F	4.1	3.4	—	6.3	21.3	64.9	559
New Zealand							
M	10.0	—	—	—	—	—	—
F	20.0	—	—	—	—	—	—
Norway							
M	16.2	4.1	—	9.1	43.2	27.4	627
F	17.6	6.3	—	14.4	35.6	26.1	568
Scotland							
M	14.7	2.6	—	3.6	39.8	39.2	771
F	15.6	4.5	—	6.7	40.0	33.3	711

Country	Smoke daily	Smoke weekly	Smoke once per week or more	Smoke less than weekly	Do not smoke (have tried)	Have never smoked	Number in sample
Sweden							
M	8.7	5.7	—	7.6	47.0	31.1	541
F	10.9	5.6	—	7.1	37.6	38.8	521
Switzerland							
M	9.5	3.6	—	10.2	35.8	40.9	279
F	10.5	4.4	—	11.3	29.3	44.4	341
U.S.A.†							
M	—	—	24.0	—	—	—	—
F	—	—	29.0	—	—	—	—
Wales							
M	13.1	2.4	—	4.4	41.9	38.2	954
F	15.1	5.2	—	4.4	41.2	34.1	1,104
Wales & Scotland							
M	—	—	18.0	—	—	—	—
F	—	—	27.0	—	—	—	—

*15–19-year-olds; †15- and 16-year-olds.
These data have been collected from a variety of studies with differing method-ologies. The WHO Cross-National Survey Statistics are courtesy of Nutbeam, N. Planning for a smoke-free generation *Smoke-free Europe:* **6**
From: *A manual on tobacco and young people for the industrialised world.* Geneva: UICC.

The development of smoking

Stages of smoking onset

Several researchers have identified a series of stages in the development of children's smoking. Although the details differ slightly between researchers, the following stages represent a distillation of the main elements.[12,13] Figure 4.3 illustrates the process.

Stage A: Pre-contemplation

Although the child may not be aware of making any decision to start smoking, factors are already operating for and against him or her doing so. The two main elements are:

(i) The child's own developmental stage;
(ii) Macro- and micro-environmental social and personal factors, for

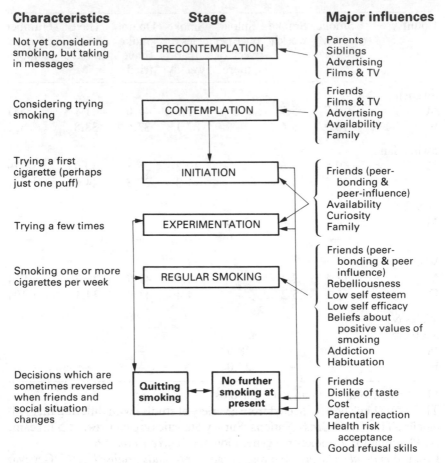

Fig. 4.3 *Stages in the development of smoking.*

example advertising, parental or friends' smoking, the security symbol of smoking such as the smell on mother's clothes, or decreasing self-esteem.

During the pre-contemplation stage, knowledge, values, beliefs and attitudes are built up and interact with social factors. Together they set the scene against which the child will or will not decide to take the step towards smoking. Numerous studies have attempted to identify the predisposing factors in a child's life and beliefs at this pre-smoking stage[13,14] (see Chapters 5 and 6).

Stage B: Contemplation
At some stage in their life most children are probably actively encouraged to try or not to try smoking. This is likely to happen more than

once in a child's life as he or she encounters new peer groups, and no specific age can therefore be allocated to this stage. At this stage the child is thinking about the pros and cons of smoking. Sometimes the first attempt at smoking occurs when a toddler picks up a cigarette from a low table and simply has a puff in imitation of parents.

Stage C: Initiation and experimentation
Initiation (trying the first cigarette) is as far as the majority of children take the smoking process. They do not take experimentation beyond the first cigarette or two either because they dislike the taste or see no positive gains in the habit. Many may however try smoking several times over a period of years.

Experimentation with smoking can start early. Pre-school children occasionally experiment with smoking and the 1990 OPCS National Survey[1] showed that 2% of the children who had tried smoking at the time of the survey had experimented before the age of 6 years. Overall, in England in 1990, one-third of pupils who had ever smoked had done so by their eleventh birthday. The peak of experimentation starts earlier for boys, at 9–12 years, than for girls at 10–13 years. By their fifth year at secondary school (15–16 years) two-thirds of school children in 1990 had at least tried a cigarette.[1]

Stage D: Regular smoking
Maintenance of smoking in young people is strongly influenced by peer bonding and peer or friends' smoking, and by either poor development of refusal skills or lack of belief in the need to refuse. The positive benefits which children with low self-esteem perceive they gain from smoking are often part of this process (see also p. 49 and Chapter 5).

There is, however, evidence to suggest that in reality the development of smoking in young people may not be explained so simply. Regular smoking in children and teenagers may take two years or more to develop,[15] with young people experimenting with smoking, becoming regular smokers and then dropping the habit before experimenting once more. It has been suggested that some young people may become addicted to smoking very quickly.[9]

Models of decision-making that relate to smoking in young people

The process of decision-making in relation to cigarette smoking is complex. Three models of health-related behaviour have been suggested which help to describe the experience.

1. The Health Belief Model[16]
In this model, a person's behaviour is related to perceptions of the risk of becoming ill as follows:

— an estimation of the seriousness of a disease

— an assessment of the likelihood of getting that disease

— the potential benefits of avoiding that disease

— the perceived costs and inconvenience involved in performing the intended behaviour (eg a teenage girl who is considering stopping smoking might gain by having more money and cleaner teeth, but might lose a boyfriend).

2. Theory of Reasoned Action[17]
According to this theory, a person's *intention* to either smoke or not is the immediate determinant of smoking. There are two key components to this intention:

(i) The *personal component* is a person's own attitude towards smoking. (Attitudes comprise belief about behaviour and an evaluation of the consequences of behaving in a certain way.)

(ii) The *socio-environmental component* is an individual's perception of how peers or friends react to that individual smoking and their views about smoking in general.

A decision to smoke or not is determined by how the personal attitudes are influenced by friends, and parental opinion.

3. Social Learning Theory[18]
In this theory, health-related behaviour change is dependent on people's beliefs about their ability to change and control their environment and health status through voluntary action (*self-efficacy*).[18,19] Emphasis is placed on the role of social modelling in which the capacity to learn by observation enables people to acquire rules and integrate patterns of behaviour based on the behaviour of others without having to form them more slowly by trial and error.

Many psychological theories which attempt to explain why people start and stop smoking were formulated before the enormous advances in communication technology. As a result they often do not take into account the increasingly powerful role that the symbolic environment, including advertising, plays in modern life. The media considerably influence patterns of thought and behaviour as well as values and attitudes. Health promotion should therefore be much more aware of the impact of the media and find ways to use it in a positive health enhancing way. How smoking is portrayed in drama, entertainment and news is as important as direct advertising and promotions.

Resisting or stopping smoking depends on personal motivation. Whereas people can easily acquire knowledge they are not necessarily motivated to act on it unless they perceive a direct benefit. Effective motivation requires short-term goals with positive incentives and minimal disincentives; long-term goals, eg reducing the risk of disease, seldom provide sufficient motivation, particularly for children. Observing that a particular type of behaviour is rewarded in a social context can be an important incentive for behavioural change. However where observed behaviour is 'punished' this is obviously a powerful disincentive to adopt that form of behaviour. Role modelling of smoking or not smoking by well known, successful and respected personalities at local and national level is therefore potentially very important to a young person considering smoking. The behaviour and attitudes of doctors, teachers, sports personalities, 'pop' stars and other 'successful' groups are therefore highly relevant.

People's judgement of their own capabilities also influences their behaviour and thought patterns. Those who judge themselves incapable of coping with new demands, for example stopping smoking, dwell upon their personal deficiencies and exaggerate potential difficulties. They thus impair their performance by diverting attention from how to change behaviour to concern over failings and mishaps. By contrast, those with a strong sense of efficacy deploy their attention and effort to the demands of the situation and are spurred by obstacles to greater effort. This has important implications for smoking. As a way of discouraging smokers, stressing the addictive nature of smoking and how difficult it is to stop may deter smokers from attempting to stop. 'It is hopeless to try', they will say.

It is well-known that children who are under-achievers and 'fed-up' with school[20] tend also to be rebellious[20,21] in that they reject authority and 'the system'. These children, whilst appearing hard and self-sufficient, often have a poor self-image and self-esteem. They are likely also to have a low self-efficacy, which makes 'refusal skills' difficult to acquire and implement.[22] Low self-efficacy makes a young person more prone to behave according to a perceived subjective norm, eg to take up smoking. A recent study found a steady decrease in girls' self-esteem, which is closely related to self-efficacy, from the first to the third years in secondary school, with a reciprocal increase in smoking prevalence.[23]

It is therefore important that smoking cessation programmes for young people take into account these personal elements. The process of building self-efficacy requires learning appropriate skills such as assertiveness and specific behaviour-change orientated skills. Although young people may not want to start smoking or to stop, unless they feel they have the skills to recognise the pressures to smoke and to know how to overcome them they are more likely to succumb to the pressures.

Skill power as against *will power* is much underdeveloped. Few young people have the single mindedness to merely 'will' themselves out of the habit of smoking. They need practical advice, support and practice in the necessary skills. Few health professionals are equipped to provide these types of skills training. Rather than giving talks to young people on the health damaging effects of smoking, it would be far better for health professionals to discuss the skills needed to give up smoking or refuse offers of cigarettes. This is developed further in Chapter 6 where various strategies of smoking intervention are considered.

In stopping smoking, as in other activities, the example set by friends and others is an important factor in building self-confidence — 'if he can do it, so can I'. Verbal persuasion and other social influences can also build self-confidence. However, fear arousal, which can destroy self-confidence, tends to be self-defeating and has no place in contemporary health promotion, and neither have doctrinaire and authoritarian attitudes amongst health professionals. If doctors and nurses are to assist with lifestyle changes they need to do so in a spirit of partnership and support rather than of judgement. Smokers, particularly young smokers, do not consider themselves ill. Therefore, the role of the 'healer' treating the sick needs to be complemented with that of a 'friend, counsellor, teacher' (which is the origin of the word *doctor*).

Applying existing models of smoking to the stages of development of smoking in young people

The main elements of the decision-making process, attitudes and beliefs and a young person's self-efficacy, probably develop at different stages in the child's life.

Two simplified models of taking decisions to smoke based on the theory of reasoned action at the age of 9 years and 13 years could therefore be those set out in Fig. 4.4.

At primary school
At primary school children go through the stage of 'concrete operations'.[24] They develop patterns of logical thought and a moral code. *Up to the age of about nine* they are anxious to avoid punishment and to gain rewards from 'important' adults.[25] At this age attempts to smoke are not based on attitudes to the habit at all, but on whether or not it can be done without punishment from their parents and other adults. *From nine to twelve years*, when many children try their first cigarette, the process has

(a) At nine years

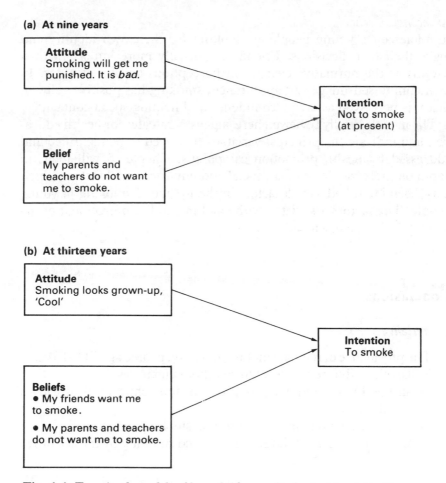

Fig. 4.4 *Two simple models of how children make the decision (a) at 9 years not to smoke, and (b) at 13 years to smoke.*

different elements. It is the 'good boy' or 'good girl' period, when children want to please others and to be very law-abiding, but it is also the time when peer groups are established, group-orientated decisions begin to operate, and curiosity is great. At this stage, the child's attitude to smoking is likely to be either (a) strong disapproval, which is both pleasing to adults and usually virtuously expressed, or (b) some approval of, or at least interest in smoking which results in experimentation. If parents smoke in the home, this will encourage children of this age that smoking is the norm. Thus any reduction in uptake of smoking in children can be approached by reducing or stopping smoking by parents.

At secondary school

In adolescence young people are looking for their own identity and make their own decisions. Friends are usually more important than parents as the normative element in perceptions and in attitudes. In maintaining self-image and appearance, smoking has positive value in that it is perceived as giving confidence and helping social contact.[26]

The models briefly reviewed here suggest strategies for health education and indicate the principal variables that need to be identified and addressed by health promotion campaigns. Chapter 5 will focus in depth on those key individual, social and environmental factors which have been identified as risk factors in the uptake of smoking in young people. The factors associated with smoking and reinforcement of the habit will also be discussed.

Conclusions

Prevalence

▓ The prevalence of regular smoking in young people aged 11–16 years is alarming. Before it is legal to sell them cigarettes:
  — in the 15-year-old age group one in four children is already a regular smoker
  — an additional one in ten children is smoking occasionally
  — only one in three children has not tried smoking by the age of 16.

Current trends

▓ The lack of any downward trend in prevalence of regular smoking in boys and girls since the early 1980s is clearly disappointing. Recent data suggest that more girls than boys now smoke.

▓ Young regular smokers are smoking on average two packets of cigarettes per week and many are consuming sufficient nicotine to become 'hooked' on the habit to the extent that they suffer withdrawal symptoms if they try to stop smoking.

Planning strategy

▓ Smoking remains a significant potential source of future health problems for young people in the UK and also in Europe (Table 4.1). Prevention and cessation of smoking which can be maintained throughout the secondary school years and into the workplace should therefore be considered major priorities for health promotion in youth.

▓ Models of the ways in which young people make decisions to smoke or not and the stages of smoking have contributed to our understanding of the development of smoking in young people. Such models assist in planning relevant, appropriate health promotion strategies.

Relation to adult smoking

▓ Because children's behaviour often matches that of their peers or adults, anti-smoking health education for young people must take place in the context of continued efforts to reduce adult smoking.

5   Personal and social factors influencing smoking

FACTS

1. Smoking in the young is directly related to adult smoking. Significant reduction in children's smoking will occur only when the role modelling of adults is considerably reduced.

2. Young regular smokers tend to be rebellious, with poor self-image, and indulge in risk-taking behaviour.

3. Parental smoking and attitudes are critically important influences on whether a child will smoke. Children are seven times less likely to smoke if they perceive strong disapproval from their parents.

4. In older children, the smoking habits of friends are important. Going against the group norm is difficult and refusal skills have to be learnt.

5. Non-smoking teachers and strict school No Smoking policies reduce cigarette consumption both in and out of school and in later life.

6. One-quarter of a million retail outlets sell tobacco in the UK, half of which break the law on sales to children.

7. Regular price increases through taxation reduce tobacco consumption whilst government tax revenue actually increases.

8. A tobacco price increase results in a greater reduction in consumption by young people than by adults. In terms of average disposable income the price of a pack of cigarettes has halved in the last 30 years.

9. The tobacco industry spends at least £72 million per year in the UK advertising and promoting cigarettes. Children smoke the currently most advertised brands.

10. A ban on tobacco advertising and sponsorship as part of a comprehensive Tobacco Act would have a significant impact on the uptake of tobacco by young people in the UK.

Factors that influence smoking

There are two kinds of study which determine the factors that influence smoking: those which determine factors at a particular point in time, and those which cover a period of time and also determine the predictors for smoking. Both types of study are important in establishing the context and environment which cause young people to smoke and the factors that reinforce the habit.

The factors that influence smoking in young people overlap and fall into two categories:

■ *Personal factors*. These concern the micro-environment in which a child grows up—ie home, friends, school, and the child's personality and self-esteem.

■ *Socio-environmental factors*. These concern the macro-environment, ie the influences exerted by the community (including employers, advertising and the media), and the government.

The factors that influence a child first to contemplate, then initiate and experiment with smoking are not necessarily the same as those associated with regular smoking. Figure 4.3 indicates some of the factors that operate at different stages. However, these stages are not discrete; they form a continuous process leading towards the take-up and habit of smoking.

PERSONAL FACTORS

The young personality

Certain characteristics have been found to be related to initiation and experimentation with smoking by children. These include risk-taking, rebelliousness, and poor self-image. To these should be added the social factors which will be discussed later. The process of 'becoming a smoker' which involves the progression from experimentation to regular smoking retains these personal factors but is susceptible to other influences.[1]

Smokers always have good reasons for smoking, at least in their own view, and the factors affecting their behaviour must be seen in this context. Jessor explained smoking as one of the several problem behaviours during the developmental transition period of adolescence.[2] He argued that such behaviour may express opposition to adult authority, provide a way of coping with anxiety, failure and frustration, express solidarity with peers and affirm personal identity. The step from experimentation to regular smoking, Jessor suggests, acts as a transition marker from adolescence to young adult status. This step suggests that smoking is seen as an adult habit. Thus, adolescent smoking is closely related to that of adults, and it might be predicted that, as adult smoking prevalence falls, so will that of adolescents. Flay suggests that the social reinforcements which adolescents obtain from smoking are the most important factors in the transition from experimentation to regular smoking.[3]

Risk-taking and rebelliousness have also been found to be associated with transition to regular smoking. Young smokers are generally socially precocious, less academically orientated, have poor refusal skills, low self-esteem and believe that smoking provides them with some positive gains.[1] Transition from experimental to regular smoking can be predicted by the perception of smoking as fun, pleasant or nice and by an expressed intention to smoke.[4] Research has shown that young 'risk-takers' in one area of behaviour tend to engage in other risky behaviours, ie associations have been found between smoking and using other drugs such as solvents, illegal drugs and alcohol[5] (see p. 27).

It has been suggested that a gap between the adolescent's aspirations and achievement may lead to role strain which may lead to stress or distress, which in turn leads to depression, self-derogation and low self-esteem; these factors might increase the risk of smoking tobacco and other drug use. Studies in the USA, using stress and coping measures, have shown that the adolescents with high stress scores are at increased risk of taking up smoking.[6,7] However, in Britain, a study in which adolescents were asked directly if they smoked to relieve stress received negative replies from two-thirds of the smokers although the young people did express a range of concerns from unemployment to examinations, and childbirth to marriage.[8]

Knowledge of the health risk of smoking plays a *relatively* small part in a child's decision about smoking and alone is insufficient to deter a child from smoking.[9,10] There are several possible reasons for this. One is that most of the serious health risks such as lung cancer, heart disease, emphysema, and the like, are perceived to be too far in the future to have real personal relevance to children.[11] Other reasons are that children do not understand the meaning of these diseases[11] and, whilst acknowledging the risks verbally, might mentally reject them. At least one study showed that regular smokers were *more* likely than non-smokers to say that smoking causes lung cancer.[12] Nevertheless, a foundation of knowledge upon which to base decision-making is essential and, in children, increased expressed knowledge of health risks has been shown to be one of the many factors associated with a decreased risk of trying smoking in the next few months.[10] It now appears that a health-risks approach combined with other methods can be effective.[13] Knowledge of the short-term or immediate physiological effects of smoking on the body are important deterrents since they are perceived by young people to be more relevant to them than long-term effects.

Home and family

Parental smoking

Parents are the source of primary socialisation and their influence is strong in the pre-school phase of children's lives.[14] This formative period affects the child's whole life. It has frequently been shown in Britain[15-18] that one or both parents' smoking is associated with smoking in their children. Girls' smoking in particular is more likely to be related to that of their mother.[8,15,17] It is not that children smoke *because* their parents smoke but, for a number of reasons including the accessibility of cigarettes, that they are at increased risk of taking up the habit.

Parental anti-smoking attitudes are strongly influential[19,20] and have been shown to carry even more weight than actual parental smoking.[19,21] In one study, children were up to seven times less likely to smoke if they perceived strong disapproval from their parents.[17]

Siblings' smoking

There is a strong correlation between the smoking habits of siblings.[15] Perhaps this is because smoking is the norm in some families and not in others. Many studies have shown even stronger links between siblings' smoking than in parent/child smoking habits.[15,21]

Family status

Socio-economic status. Although there is much higher smoking prevalence among adults in manual socio-economic groups, no social class differences have been observed in the prevalence of smoking in British children and teenagers.[8,10,15] This may be because friendships in school cross socio-economic boundaries or because children of manual socio-economic groups might have less pocket money with which to purchase cigarettes.[22] When children become employed their purchasing power increases and teenage smokers have been shown to be more likely than non-smokers to have part-time jobs outside school.[23]

Lone parent status has been shown to be associated with an increased smoking prevalence in adults.[24,25] One study showed that the older teenage daughters of lone parents also had an increased risk of being smokers, especially if their mothers smoked.[26] However, studies have shown that this increased likelihood applies whether or not the lone mother is a smoker.[26,27]

Ethnicity

A major study amongst over 10,000 school children aged between 9 and 15 years throughout England[28] indicated that white children were most likely to be regular smokers (6%) compared with 2% of Afro-Caribbean and 2% of Asian children who said they smoked regularly. Experimentation is similar for white (32%) and Afro-Caribbean children (30%) but significantly lower among Asian children (20%).[28]

Religion

Some religions or religious groups (eg Islam and Seventh Day Adventists) actually forbid smoking, while others (eg Roman Catholicism) do not..At present, Asian children, especially Moslems, are less likely to smoke than are other children.[29] As a deterrent to smoking, religious observance in itself may be more relevant than belonging to a particular religious faith. The more frequently children attend religious services, the less likely they are to smoke.[30] However, as children become integrated into mixed peer groups, religious boundaries may also be crossed and smoking become the norm.

Deprivation

Children with emotional and behavioural difficulties have a very high smoking prevalence. They are often supported and encouraged in their smoking by carers, who use cigarettes as part of a reward system for improved behaviour. It has also been shown that teenagers in the USA between the ages of fourteen to seventeen years who have been abused are three times more likely to smoke than non-abused youngsters.[31]

Friends and social life

Friends' smoking

Although the family has the first impact on the child, as he or she grows older the influence of friends becomes extremely strong. Three major longitudinal studies in the UK[8,10,15] have shown that best friends' smoking is one of the most important factors related to the uptake of smoking. Another has shown that having a boyfriend or girlfriend, particularly if he or she is a smoker, is a predictor.[32] Only one major longitudinal study has not included some aspect of friendship as a major predictor of smoking.[33] Studies in the USA have also found best friends' smoking to be of importance.[34,35]

The influence appears to operate in two ways, as peer influence and peer-bonding. In the first instance, children who smoke in primary school encourage, or even frighten, others into trying a cigarette, and secondly, young smokers often have much in common and tend to team up as peer groups. Therefore having friends who smoke can act as a predictor and as a reinforcer of the habit.

The opinion of friends is important to children.[8,10,15] The influence of friends is also linked with status. Children do not want to be seen by their friends as being 'wimps'. Non-smokers report that their friends made fun of them if they did not smoke.[30] Many obtain their first cigarette from a friend and young smokers often associate with older peer groups, boyfriends or girlfriends.[16] Being offered a cigarette by friends is particularly important. Refusing can go against the group norm and refusal skills need to be learned. In this case their smoking is likely to be not only for conformity but also to increase their appearance of maturity.

Friends have also been shown to influence young smokers to become non-smokers.[36] A change of friend can mean a change of smoking habit.

Social activities

Leisure activities such as dancing, going to discos and parties and having friends of the opposite sex are all associated with smoking.[23]

School

Teachers' smoking

Whilst few children see their teachers as role models, most children probably view them as figures of authority. Thus a smoking teacher legitimises the habit and endorses its acceptability as an adult activity for the child.[37] This may, of course, simply reflect a generally more permissive attitude to smoking in such schools.

Schools and school policy

One study has shown that schools and colleges with a No Smoking policy for both staff and students have fewer smokers and less smoking among students.[38] This study also showed that when students were not allowed to smoke, 20% of the over-16s were regular smokers, as against 32% when they could smoke. The difference was even greater when staff also were not permitted to smoke, ie 16% as against 34%. The students did not appear to make up their nicotine level outside college hours. When they could smoke in college the average number of cigarettes smoked per week in college was 17, and outside was 28, as against 5 inside and 18 outside for non-smoking colleges. In addition, these benefits may continue since another study has shown a lower smoking prevalence among former students of a school with a strict policy than among those from a more permissive school.[39] Lack of school uniforms and lack of discipline in school have been associated with increased prevalence of smoking.[40]

Few data exist on schools' smoking policies in the UK. According to the Health Education Authority, research indicates that few schools in England have written policies, though most have informal regulations; and few are completely smoke-free. In 1991, Birmingham City Council Education Department announced a policy to make all schools, sixth form colleges and offices non-smoking areas (with specially designated smoking rooms in some circumstances) from 1 January 1992, to be extended to include colleges of further education thereafter.[41]

SOCIAL INFLUENCES ON SMOKING

Smoking in public places

The extent to which smoking is allowed in public places is closely related to the social acceptability of smoking, which the cigarette manufacturers think holds the key to the continued existence of their market. In 1979, a tobacco industry executive, reviewing a speech on tobacco and disease by the then Director-General of the World Health Organisation, concluded that it confirmed the industry's own analysis that 'the social acceptability issue will be the central battleground on which our case in the long run will be lost or won.' [42]

After learning that the industry saw this area of policy as the one most likely to reduce sales—and hence future disease—public health campaigners stepped up their efforts to increase the provision of non-smoking areas in public places. A major boost to their efforts was provided during the 1980s by studies demonstrating that prolonged exposure to other people's smoke gives non-smokers an increased risk of lung cancer. In 1991, 48 leading medical and health organisations put their names to a booklet reviewing the scientific evidence of the health effects of passive smoking, concluding that risk was proven in a number of areas, including lung cancer and childhood respiratory disease.[43]

The most recent report on smoking by this College, published in 1983,[44] stated that the aim in this particular area of public health policy must be to create a society in which non-smoking is the norm, with smoking areas designated where necessary and convenient, rather than the reverse.[44] There is no doubt that the rate of change in this direction has been faster in the last few years than at any previous time, although smoking in public places still remains the norm despite the fact that less than one-third of British adults are smokers. As long as role models continue to smoke in public, young people will perceive that smoking is normal adult behaviour. For this reason this report has included smoking in public, including the workplace.

The workplace

The greatest progress in restricting smoking has been made at the workplace. Non-smoking employees who are not protected by a No Smoking policy may be exposed to their colleagues' smoke for seven to eight hours every working day. As the risks of long-term exposure to other people's smoke have become better known, there has been increasing demand among non-smokers to work in smoke-free environments. Smokers themselves seem to agree with this demand: in 1987, 90% of non-smokers and 81% of smokers agreed that people who do not smoke should have the right to work in air free from tobacco smoke.[45]

The majority of employers have implemented some sort of restrictions on smoking at work. An unpublished survey in 1990 by the Institute of Directors indicated that only about 11% of employers allowed completely unrestricted smoking at work; and 28% had introduced formal policies. In the same year, a MORI survey of Britain's top 500 companies found that one in five had total bans, half of them imposed within the year.[46] In another survey in 1990, 59% of adults in employment reported that there were restrictions on smoking at their places of work.[47] A rapid acceleration in the move to smoke-free workplaces could follow a successful prosecution of an employer under health and safety legislation.

Health service premises

Unfortunately, hospitals and other health service premises have been slow to act. In 1985, the Department of Health and Social Security issued Health Circular HC(85)22: 'Health services management: promoting non-smoking on NHS premises'. Surveys in England in 1987 and 1988 found that while most district health authorities (DHAs) had a written policy, many had not progressed beyond this statement of intent, omitting to define implementation and monitoring procedures. Those which did have policies had tended to delegate responsibility to personnel who were powerless to enforce them.

A British Medical Association survey reviewing progress in Scotland from 1985 to 1989 found there had been good progress by Health Boards in the production of written policies and in the provision of smoke-free areas in NHS premises, with the important exception of wards and day rooms.

The Health Education Authority, which published a review of the English surveys, recommended that the Department of Health issue a new circular requesting DHAs to designate limited smoking areas for staff and for patients, so that non smokers are never exposed to smoke; this should be achieved within a specified period of time, with the DHAs being provided with guidelines on implementation and monitoring; and the long-term aim should be the total elimination of smoking on NHS premises, with exemption for long-stay patients only.[48] As yet, the Department of Health has not acted on these recommendations.

Local authorities

As employers of large numbers of people and as managers of many public buildings, sports and leisure facilities, local authorities have both a special responsibility and a major opportunity to protect the health of non-smokers. Nevertheless, only half of the district councils in England have a formal policy on smoking at work; and councils are not using their influence sufficiently to help create smoke-free public places. As in so many other areas of smoking policy, a stronger lead from central government is required.[49]

Leisure and travel industries

Restaurants and hotels have been much slower to provide smoke-free accommodation than their counterparts in North America. Nevertheless, change is now taking place; the Action on Smoking and Health (ASH) 1992 guide to restaurants, hotels and bed and breakfast establishments listed over 1,500 which provided some form of smoke-free accommodation, compared with only 244 which could be found for its 1984 guide. Some of the larger hotel chains routinely cite their smoke-free facilities in advertisements.

Most large cinema chains have followed art cinemas in making their auditoria totally smoke-free, although smoking is still allowed in cinema foyers.

Many public transport authorities have introduced entirely smoke-free travel. These include London Transport buses and underground trains, all domestic flights on British Airways and many commuter trains operating short journeys to and from major cities. Some small airlines operating in Europe (eg Air UK) and international airlines (eg Air Canada's transatlantic flights) operate a total ban on smoking in their aeroplanes. The USA has now enacted a law that makes all domestic flights smoke-free.

Government policy on smoking in public

In the USA, the US Surgeon General and the Environmental Protection Agency have declared passive smoking to be a proven health hazard and legislation setting minimum standards for the protection of non-smokers has been enacted by many States. In addition, many Federal organisations and employers have introduced their own non-smoking policies even if not required by law. In the UK, however, while the government has acknowledged the risks of passive smoking, it has consistently refused to legislate to provide a minimum level of protection in any areas.

At the end of 1991, the Department of the Environment launched a code of practice on smoking in public places, providing guidance for owners and managers of places visited by the public.[50] Significantly, this pamphlet recognises that people have a right to breathe air unpolluted by tobacco smoke, that environmental smoke is a health hazard and that non-smoking should be the norm in buildings frequented by the public, with special provision for smoking where appropriate. While the code of practice lacks legislative backing, it is at least a step in the right direction; and its principles should be used as the basis of legislation in the future. Such legislation should cover workplaces.

Availability of tobacco

The sheer size of the cigarette market is daunting: in the UK in 1990 some 14 million smokers[51] bought 93 billion cigarettes at a total cost of £7.6 billion.[52] One brand alone accounted for sales of £1.3 billion; and four other leading brands made up a further £2 billion. Cigarettes form the fourth largest consumer market, after clothing, beer and meat.[53]

One of the major problems for public health workers who try to reduce tobacco consumption is the extent to which smoking is ingrained in the British way of life. This includes the widespread availability of cigarettes and other tobacco goods. Although purchased by less than one-third of adults, cigarettes are sold by around a quarter of a million retail outlets, the main type being independent confectioners, news-agents and tobacconists, who handle just over a quarter of all sales.

Sales to children

A large number of retailers still break the law which prohibits the sale of cigarettes to children under sixteen. Shops are by far the leading source of cigarette supply for child smokers—almost three-quarters of children who smoke regularly buy cigarettes from a shop at least once a week;[54] and around 50% of retailers sell cigarettes to obviously underage children.[55] Concern about illegal sales to children has led to increases in the fines for convicted offenders in recent years, as well as to efforts to educate retailers and the public. While there has been a rise in the number of prosecutions, it is still under one hundred each year, representing less than one in a thousand retailers who break the law.[56] It remains to be seen whether the most recent changes, involving new legislation passed in 1991 raising the maximum fine further, clarifying other aspects of the law and requiring local authorities to review its enforcement, will result in greater compliance. In the meantime, there are growing demands from health organisations for the return of a system of retail licensing.

There are two sides to the question of setting an age limit for the sale of cigarettes. On the one hand there is the fear that this age limit could reinforce the adult image of smoking and the attraction of 'forbidden fruit'. Alternatively, making cigarettes less available to children should make it more difficult for them to smoke.

Despite their obvious need to recruit young people into cigarette smoking, the tobacco companies adopt a public posture of concern about illegal sales to children and they claim their support for govern-ment policy in this area. They have even persuaded health ministers to involve them in retailer education campaigns as part of the 'voluntary agreements' on tobacco advertising. However, less than 20% of shops selling tobacco display the industry's warning of the law on sales. Those few notices that are on display are small and are overwhelmed by the quantity of cigarette advertising carried on shop fronts and doorways.

Price

Price is one of the most important factors affecting cigarette consump-tion, at least in the short term (Figure 5.1). The relationship between

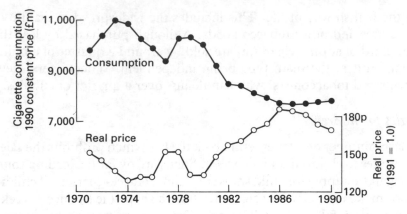

Fig. 5.1 *The relationship between the price of cigarettes and consumption, 1971–90. Both variables are adjusted for inflation.* (By permission of Joy Townsend, Medical Research Council Epidemiology and Medical Care Unit).

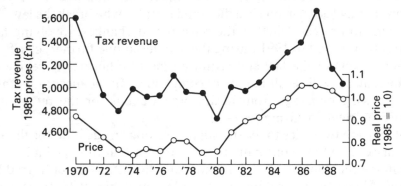

Fig. 5.2 *The relationship between the price of cigarettes and tax revenue, 1970–89. Both variables are adjusted for inflation.* (By permission of Joy Townsend, Medical Research Council Epidemiology and Medical Care Unit).

real price and consumption is very close, with an elasticity of around −0.5: this means that a 1% rise in price causes a decline in consumption of 0.5%.[57] Studies in North America show that a price increase results in a greater reduction in consumption in young people than in adults.[58]

Fortunately, this type of relationship between price and consumption allows the government to increase the Exchequer's revenue by raising tobacco tax: it still receives more tax from the smaller number of cigarettes sold at the new, higher rate than it loses from those who give up or cut down their smoking after the rise. This is illustrated in Fig. 5.2 and argues against the commonly held theory that dependence on tax revenue inhibits government action to reduce consumption, as does the declining importance of tobacco tax as a source of revenue during the second half of the century.[59]

In 1948 tobacco tax accounted for approximately 16% of total government current revenue; by 1968 this had halved to 8%; and by 1985 it had halved again to form only 4% of total revenue.[59] However, tobacco tax revenue can be maintained in real terms by increasing the rate of tobacco tax, since the rise in rate more than offsets the fall in consumption. Theoretically, there will be a point of diminishing returns, when tobacco taxation will be so high and so many smokers give up that total revenue will decrease. However, it is unlikely that tobacco will be more than a minor source of Treasury revenue by the time this point is reached.

Tobacco products are included in the retail price index. At times of high inflation, there is a strong disincentive to raise tobacco tax because this will fuel inflation. This compromises the ability of the Chancellor to increase tobacco tax for health reasons. The UK government has been pressed for some time to remove tobacco from the retail price index; in this it would follow the lead of France, Portugal and Luxembourg.

Despite fairly regular tax increases over the last decade and a half, the real price of cigarettes still remains less than it was in 1948. Furthermore, when expressed in terms of average disposable income, cigarettes have become increasingly affordable, even during times of price rises. As a percentage of average gross weekly wages for adult male manual workers in manufacturing industries, the price of an average pack of 20 cigarettes has halved in the last thirty years. The figures for October 1961, 1971, 1981 and 1990 were 1.4%, 0.9%, 0.8% and 0.7% respectively.[60]

Smoking a cigarette is a cheap activity compared to other things which non-smokers may do on the same sort of occasions when smokers light up. At the end of 1991, an average cigarette cost about 10p. This compared with 15–40p for a typical snack or confectionery bar, 35–50p for a soft drink and 50p–£1.20 for a half unit of alcohol.

Tobacco and the EC

Tobacco tax rates vary significantly across the EC and several years of negotiation failed to find an acceptable uniform tax rate for all member states. Instead, a minimum level has been agreed which will raise cigarette prices in the countries with lower tobacco tax rates (eg Greece, Spain) whilst in theory leaving the higher-taxing countries, including the UK, free to increase tax further. However, the freedom to raise tax levels is limited by the single market and the division of tax liability between flat rate and proportional tax makes this a complex issue. The common agriculture policy of the European Community subsidises tobacco production by some £988 million per annum. This policy, which was intended to maintain farmers' incomes and adapt production to demand, has spiralled out of control. In fact, the EC is now the world's largest importer of raw tobacco, while exporting greatly increased crops of virtually unmarketable varieties to countries in Central and Eastern Europe, North Africa and the Middle East. The EC spends only about £7 million per annum on the Europe Against Cancer programme.[61]

Tobacco promotion

In this section, the term promotion is used to cover all forms of advertising, including sponsorship and the development of lines of other goods and services carrying cigarette brand names. Since manufactured cigarettes so dominate the UK market, figures and examples deal exclusively with cigarette promotion.

The main purpose of cigarette promotion is to deliver to a target group of smokers or potential smokers a message which will encourage them to make repeated purchases of the brand. The main effects of advertising are not instantaneous, but probably occur after a long time lag. Much cigarette advertising theory involves the concept of 'myth', meaning the use of a story, theme or type of character that appeals to a group of people by embodying their cultural ideals or by giving expression to their emotions.

A classic myth used in some cigarette advertising is the cowboy—free, independent, self-sufficient and not bullied by authority; a more modern version is the motor racing driver, with his courage, daring and virility. Embodying such figures in cigarette promotional material may satisfy the target group by acknowledging and reflecting some of their self-perceived qualities or by answering their fantasies. When purchasing a particular brand, therefore, they are to some extent identifying themselves as a particular type of person. Exhaustive research enables cigarette advertisers to identify the myths and the settings which most appeal to their targets, and to develop distinctive names, colours and logos for their brands which are persistently associated with those qualities. A constant stream of messages from the resulting advertisements, promotional activities and pack designs helps them to recruit new smokers; and it reinforces brand loyalty among their existing customers, offering reassurance to counter any doubts, such as health worries.

All cigarettes are intrinsically the same: tubes of paper with chopped dried leaves inside which, when ignited, produce smoke containing several thousand chemicals, many of them highly toxic. By any reasonable assessment, therefore, there are no significant, positive qualities which can be associated truthfully with the most dangerous consumer product the world has ever known, one which is not only highly addictive to many users, but which causes more premature deaths than all other known, avoidable causes put together and for which there is no safe level of consumption. Indeed, the cigarette is unique in being the only consumer product which is highly dangerous simply when used as intended by the manufacturers. The emergence and dissemination of knowledge about the unparalleled dangers of smoking has given the cigarette advertiser an additional task: to try to negate health messages about smoking.

Since the publication of the first report of the Royal College of Physicians on smoking and health,[62] there has been increasing demand for all forms of tobacco promotion to be banned. This has come not just from the medical and health professions, with over thirty organisations now calling for a ban,[63] but from many other organisations and individuals as well. Among the general public, 71% of UK adults now favour banning all cigarette advertising.[64]

Governments and Ministers of all sides are subjected to massive political lobbying by the tobacco industry. A number of Members of Parliament are paid by the tobacco and advertising industries to represent their interests in Parliament. Other Members of Parliament side with the tobacco industry simply for reasons of political belief. Health Ministers not supported by clear Cabinet policy have made ineffective efforts to curb tobacco promotion when faced with lobbying on such a scale. This has resulted in weak voluntary agreements with the tobacco companies which should more accurately be described as negotiated agreements. These involve a promise by the companies to abide by a certain set of rules for a fixed period of time in return for a promise by the Government to take no further action during that time. The complexities of the voluntary agreements mean that members of the public are rarely sufficiently knowledgeable to make successful complaints about breaches of the agreement. The agreements are in fact so permissive that breaches are few and usually accidental.

Children

One of the factors which influences smoking in children is advertising. The tobacco industry asserts that it does not want children to smoke and that cigarette advertising is aimed at adult smokers to encourage brand switching.[65] Nevertheless, children are very aware of cigarette advertisements; they like them, and can interpret at least some of the messages.[66] The advertisers' aims of associating individual cigarette brands with special logos, colours and typefaces to circumvent advertising restrictions, seems to work well: when shown an advertisement for 'JPS Grand Prix Holidays' which did not carry a health warning, 91% of 12 to 16-year-olds said it advertised cigarettes.[67]

Non-smoking children with favourite cigarette advertisements have been shown to hold more positive views about smoking than those with no favourite advertisement,[68] and children aged 12 who approve of cigarette advertising are twice as likely to become smokers within a year as children who disapprove of it.[69] In addition, cigarette advertising has been found to encourage smoking in teenagers by reinforcing the adolescent's image of him- or herself as successful, witty, exciting and/ or glamorous.[70] Although the voluntary agreement protects young readers from cigarette advertising in their own publications, many young people read their parents' magazines,[71] as well as being exposed to cigarette promotion through television coverage of sponsored events, billboards and many other media. The success of advertising to children is illustrated by a study which showed the four currently most heavily advertised brands were the four most popular brands for children (Benson & Hedges, Embassy, Silk Cut, Marlboro) but not all of them for adults (MORI-HEA Survey). Adults tend to stay loyal to brands which were heavily promoted in their youth (eg John Player Special). Similar results have been found elsewhere, eg in the USA.[72]

Although cigarette commercials do not appear on television in the United Kingdom, children still think they see them, either by mistaking cigar, pipe tobacco or anti-smoking advertisements (the two former categories were banned in 1991 under EC regulations), or in films, soap operas or sports sponsorship publicity. Glamour, sophistication, slimness and relief from tension are all portrayed.[73,74] 'Fashion' may have an important role to play in promoting smoking in youth.

The voluntary agreement system is supposed to protect children by prohibiting advertisements showing images such as lively, healthy, successful, young people smoking, but children are still exposed to large amounts of promotion linking smoking with these positive images through the sponsorship of sports and other activities. The agreement also prevents cigarette advertisements from appearing in magazines with a female readership of 200,000 or more, of whom at least one quarter are aged between 15 and 24 years, but the sponsorship of fashion events, promotional activities at discos and placement of cigarettes in films and other advertisements effectively circumvent this provision. For example, Philip Morris paid $42,000 to have Marlboro featured in 'Superman II'—patently a young person's film. In the film, contrary to the comic-book characterisation, Lois Lane smokes incessantly.[75]

Regulation: the current UK position

The tobacco industry resists advertising bans more vigorously than any other measures; and conversely, it always seeks to praise the 'voluntary agreement' system when threatened with a ban. This in itself is perhaps the strongest evidence for the effectiveness of a ban in reducing consumption. The main shortcomings of 'voluntary agreements' are that they tend to be highly selective in nature, omitting many types of promotional activity. They involve different government departments, some pulling in opposite directions from others. The agreement is adjudicated by a committee half of which comprises tobacco industry representatives and is therefore interpreted very laxly. In the circumstances, the companies have little to lose by pushing their interpretations to the limits—and sometimes beyond. The many rounds of meetings with ministers, officials and advertising industry bodies mean that negotiations for new agreements can take a matter of years, allowing plenty of time for the companies to plan how to circumvent the restrictions about to be agreed. The Department of Health, as one of the parties to the agreement, is effectively neutralised. Instead of playing for health and initiating policy changes, the Department is forced into the position of referee between health on the one side and the tobacco industry on the other.

Sports sponsorship

The most outrageous and deplorable example of circumvention of the voluntary agreement on cigarette advertising is the existence of massive cigarette brand promotions by means of sports sponsorship. Clauses in the agreement between the manufacturers and the Department of Health specifically prohibit advertisements associating cigarettes with success in sport. Other clauses prohibit association with certain qualities often found in sports, such as motor racing, for example courage, daring or virility, or with heroes of the young or with young people themselves. To get round these restrictions, the cigarette companies sponsor sporting and cultural events, especially those which are shown on television (eg motor racing, snooker, cricket); or events which attract a young audience (eg discos). In the words of one cigarette company's head of motor racing activities: 'What we wanted was to promote a particular image of adventure, of courage, of virility.'[76]

Tobacco industry secrecy prevents an accurate and up-to-date figure for total expenditure on cigarette promotion. Regular advertising totals over £67m per annum[77] and sports sponsorship of £5.3m per annum[78] have been declared, but this excludes substantial sums spent 'below the line', including large-scale advertising campaigns purporting to promote sporting events sponsored by a cigarette brand, but clearly intended primarily to advertise the brand itself. The amount spent on sponsorship does not fully represent the massive exposure achieved in circumvention of the voluntary agreement, being so much cheaper than the cost of purchasing equivalent exposure by means of regular television advertising. On average, television coverage of cigarette-sponsored sporting events amounts to an hour per day, virtually all of it on the BBC channels.

Sports sponsorship is not only the most widespread and blatant way the advertising agreement is breached, but it is actually recognised officially and enshrined in its own 'voluntary agreement', this time between the tobacco manufacturers and the Minister for Sport. This underlines the importance of developing an overall government policy on smoking, rather than a Department of Health policy which may cut across the interests of other government Departments.

Banning tobacco promotion

Nineteen countries now have total bans on all forms of tobacco promotion and many more have partial bans.[79] In several states of Australia, for example, most forms of tobacco promotion are banned and an extra tax has been levied on cigarettes to generate a special fund which pays for health promotion, medical and health research and funding for sports and cultural events. This is an incentive to break the domination of tobacco sponsorship and to enable such events to promote healthy messages instead of smoking. Legislation has been announced which will ban all forms of promotion in all Australian states.

Advertising a dangerous product for which there is considerable uptake among young people is clearly unethical. However, there is in addition good evidence that tobacco promotion bans do help reduce smoking. In a study examining tobacco consumption in 22 OECD countries between 1960 and 1986, it was found that since 1973 tobacco advertising restrictions had increasingly been associated with lower consumption.[80]

Norway introduced a ban on tobacco advertising as long ago as 1975 on a purely ethical basis. The prevalence of smoking in children had been increasing steadily over the previous two decades, but after the ban it decreased steadily, even at a time when the real price of cigarettes was falling (17% in 1975 down to 10% in 1990 of 13–15-year-olds).[81]

Canada introduced a wide range of measures including an advertising ban in January 1989 at a time when overall tobacco consumption had been falling steadily since 1982. After the ban was introduced, the rate of decline in consumption doubled from an average 3.6% per annum to 7.6% in 1989 and 6.7% in 1990. In 1990, the real tobacco price increased by 8.9% compared to an average annual price rise for 1983 to 1988 of 8.6%, and thus it is unlikely to be responsible for the increased rate of decline in tobacco consumption.[82]

New Zealand introduced an advertising ban as part of a model Tobacco Act in December 1990, over a period when there was little change in the real price of tobacco. (New Zealand tobacco tax is adjusted twice yearly in parallel with the retail price index). Immediately prior to the advertising ban, spending on cigarette advertising rose by 14% and was associated with an increase in consumption of 4%, and of prevalence from 26.8% to 27.5% in adults at a time when the real price of tobacco actually increased by 4%. Following the introduction of the advertising ban, tobacco consumption was 11.3% lower in the first 6 months of 1991 (after the ban) compared with the first 6 months of 1990, despite there being no other relevant changes to affect consumption. Almost one in 11 smokers gave up smoking after the introduction of the model Tobacco Act.[82] (For an example of a model tobacco policy, see Appendix 4.)

Following the New Zealand data, the UK Department of Health, which had previously accepted the tobacco industry line that the evidence was inconclusive, was reported in early 1992 to have accepted an internal report concluding that a ban on tobacco promotion would help reduce smoking.[83]

A draft Directive on Tobacco Advertising produced by the Commission of the European Community, and passed by the European Parliament in February 1991, proposing a complete ban on all forms of tobacco promotion, has been resisted by the tobacco industry with the aid of a number of Member States' governments, including the British government. Similar Directives on health warnings and on tar reduction have already been passed, breaking the mould of voluntary arrangements for tobacco control policy in Britain.

Conclusions

Influence of friends and parents

▨ Parents', teachers' and friends' smoking, friends' approval of smoking, perception of what friends think about smoking and holding a positive attitude towards smoking are all key influences in the uptake of smoking in childhood and adolescence.

Social factors

■ Smoking appears to perform an important 'social' function for young people and provides a readily accessible and relatively inexpensive means of social barter and bonding. Young people are well aware of the health hazards of smoking; however, they perceive that benefits in social terms outweigh the perceived potential health problems.

Availability and advertising

■ Smoking in young people is reinforced and maintained by a number of factors in the immediate and wider social environment, particularly the availability of cigarettes to young people and tobacco advertising. A ban on tobacco advertising would have a significant impact on the uptake of tobacco by young people in the UK.

Restriction of smoking

■ Ensuring the establishment of non-smoking as the norm in society and the removal of the omnipresence of tobacco promotion appear to be crucial to the prevention and cessation of smoking in the longer term.

6 Intervention strategies

Introduction

Since the publication of the previous Royal College of Physicians report in 1983 the concept of setting targets for health gain has been introduced into health planning in the UK. Measurable indicators of health status have been selected and improvements have been proposed for specified time periods. Ambitious smoking targets, including targets for young people, have now been set for England,[1] Scotland[2] and Wales[3] and accountability and review mechanisms are being established to ensure progress. But how will the smoking targets be achieved?

This chapter discusses the types of interventions available for reducing the prevalence of smoking among young people, drawing on the evidence presented in Chapters 4 and 5. The various approaches will be considered under the headings used in the Ottawa Charter for Health Promotion,[4] the more effective of which are summarised in Tables 1–5. The development of overarching healthy public policy is considered the major priority but for reasons of context and comprehension it is discussed at the end of this chapter.

DEVELOP PERSONAL SKILLS

Table 1   **Strategies to develop personal skills**

- **Provide relevant information on the short- and long-term impact of teenage smoking on physical fitness, health, personal expenditure, appearance, environment, the economy and society as a whole;**

- **Assist young people to resist the social and marketing pressures to smoke by teaching appropriate personal and social skills in schools;**

- **Construct programmes to match the stage of development of the smoking habit, using new and innovative teaching methods;**

- **Use primary and secondary schools as an efficient setting in which to deliver educational programmes to large numbers of young people;**

- **Use different methods of communication, combining personal, group and mass media methods to reach all young people, including high risk groups.**

Improve knowledge

When the health hazards of smoking became known in the 1950s and
1960s smoking education programmes largely concentrated on providing information to people. Often a 'guest' health professional such as
a doctor was invited to give a talk at schools. However, such didactic
teaching approaches have consistently been shown to be ineffective in
influencing smoking behaviour.[5] It is disappointing therefore that such
an unsophisticated approach is still in common use in many schools and
may be one reason for the poor progress on the prevention of teenage
smoking. However, over the past decade there have been an increasing
number of reports of more promising smoking education programmes.
These have been based on new approaches to teaching and a better
understanding of how the teaching curriculum can be used.[6]

A large number of smoking education projects based on improving
young people's knowledge have now been developed for schools. These
are commonly aimed at younger pupils where the development of a
good knowledge base is seen as essential. The Health Belief Model
(Chapter 4) suggests that to make a positive health decision it is
necessary first to understand how the body works and how smoking
affects it. An important feature of many programmes has been the
development of classroom approaches which are based on discussion
and discovery, for example the Life Education Centres Project which is
being piloted in Welsh primary schools.

The most widely distributed in the UK is the 'My Body' project[7]
which is a knowledge-based programme for 9–11-year-olds. Developed
initially by the Health Education Council from the Berkeley Project in
the USA it appears to have a beneficial effect on knowledge and attitude,
and to reduce experimental smoking. However, factually based programmes are not in themselves sufficient to effect reductions in teenage
smoking long term. This is because of the very powerful influences in
society which encourage smoking. Adolescents, like older people, do
not always do what they know they should do. Young people are greatly
influenced by a range of social 'pressures' to smoke from their peers,
their families and through advertising,[8] as was outlined in Chapter 5.

Resist social pressures

As a result of these observations,[8] 'person-centred' rather than 'sub-
stance-centred' education programmes have been devised which focus
on the development of personal and social skills. Smoking, like an
infectious disease, can be caught, and it can also be taught by others.
The aim therefore is to 'immunise' young people against such social

pressures before they are seriously ex osed to them,[9] especially before the ages of maximum recruitment to smoking (13–15 years).

For example, the Finnish North Karelia Youth Project, like the US programmes, used older pupils in the teaching process, and focussed on skills-training to help 10–13-year-olds resist social pressures to smoke.[10] The Oslo Youth Study incorporated a similar approach.[11] Both these programmes achieved significant reductions in tobacco use among the children studied compared with a reference group who did not receive the programme. However, it should be emphasised that these projects, like those in the USA on which they were modelled, were undertaken in 'ideal' classroom situations.

A great variety of curriculum packages, visual aids etc, ultimately derived from the 'resist social pressures' principles, are now in use in the UK.[12] The 'Smoking and Me' project, for example, is considered by teachers to be useful and innovative, but few are optimistic about its impact.[13] Nevertheless, Glynn[14] and Cullen[15] consider that the use of school health education programmes can result in a worthwhile 5–10 percentage point reduction in prevalence at age 16 years, compared to controls. While the effects may diminish in schools remote from the original test sites,[16] a statistically significant effect still remains.[17] The benefits may last for five years, ie up to age 16–18 years, but eventually 'wash out',[18,19] leaving no visible difference with controls who are themselves exposed to a wider range of smoking control measures. However, it cannot be assumed that these promising results can be replicated in 'normal' schools within the British state system. Further studies are required to test the effectiveness of education programmes in real life situations.

Few studies report success in helping young people to stop once the smoking habit is established after the age of 14 years. It is, of course, possible that teenagers who delay taking up smoking because of school programmes may quit earlier. The converse is known to occur, ie those who start early are least likely to stop in later life.[19]

Devise effective curricula

Much remains to be done to identify the most valuable attributes of school smoking prevention programmes.[20] However, Bellew and Wayne,[21] in a recent review, recommend that the curriculum content of effective approaches should include:

— information on both the short- and long-term health consequences of smoking

— exploration of social influences, ie parents, peers and the media
  (eg advertising)

— correction of adolescents' tendency to over-estimate smoking especially
  among their peers

— development of skills to resist the pressure to smoke from others

— development of coping strategies to replace smoking as a habit

— emphasis on differing gender needs and on promoting a positive image of
  the non-smoker

Active participation by pupils—perhaps involving some measure of
peer leadership—is also recommended. Support from parents is helpful
at all ages, but active involvement of parents is best avoided beyond the
age of 11–12 years. Finally, Bellew and Wayne consider that smoking
education can be taught separately or as part of a more general health
education course—provided that the smoking-specific elements are not
neglected.

The acceptability of smoking education in schools is no longer in
question, especially since it now forms part of the statutory National
Curriculum and the non-statutory cross-curricular theme of health
education. Costs will vary according to the need for introductory and
maintenance training, and much will depend on whether they fall on the
local education authority, the school or the NHS. The biggest challenge
that still remains is to develop methods that are effective in real life
classroom situations. A worrying feature is the growing problem of
smoking amongst girls, leading to adult smoking. Further research and
development work is still needed.

CREATE SUPPORTIVE ENVIRONMENTS

Table 2   **Strategies to create supportive environments**

▓ **Develop a social climate of opinion which promotes non-smoking as the
norm by reducing current adult smoking as a primary objective;**

▓ **Promote non-smoking, and use legislation and regulation to severely
restrict smoking in public places, particularly where young people
congregate;**

▓ **Involve the family and parents in smoking education to reinforce teaching in the classroom;**

▓ **Implement school and youth club policies on smoking control for staff as
well as pupils, and provide better training for teachers and youth-
workers.**

Involve the family

The family, and parents in particular, are an important influence on smoking behaviour (Chapter 5). Many of the 'social skills' schools projects, for example North Karelia,[10] invite consultation with parents, but do not use the home as part of the main teaching structure. In Norway more deliberate attempts to involve parents actively in smoking education have resulted in important reductions in pupils' tobacco consumption, compared with a reference group.[22] This project was adapted for use in schools in the UK by the Health Education Council as the 'Family Smoking Education Project'. Teachers find it a useful teaching aid and one that captures the interest of pupils.[23]

A family linked programme developed for use with younger pupils (9–10 years) in the UK[24] has recently also reported very positive results. 'The Brigantia Smoking Prevention Programme' is a three-stage smoking education project which has been designed for use at three critical stages in the development of smoking behaviour: 9–11 years when early experimentation begins; 12–13 years when there is a marked increase in regular smoking; and 15–16 years when many young people wish to stop smoking. Evaluation of the first stage has shown that experimental smoking can be reduced, and that parents can be reached and influenced by their children.[25] Boys' fathers' smoking prevalence fell from 38% to 30% over four months but there was no effect on mothers or girls' fathers. There have been similar findings in the United States.[26]

Reduce adult smoking

Sadly, none of the child-orientated interventions described above have been shown to have a permanent effect on teenage smoking prevalence. Fortunately, however, adult smoking is falling. Goddard[27] considers that: 'As smoking continues to decline among the adult population, fewer children will be brought up in homes where smoking is considered acceptable, and this in itself will contribute to the reduction in the proportion of children who start to smoke.'

It is therefore not surprising that the fall in teenage smoking in the USA has followed, and not led, the major decline in adult prevalence since 1960.[28] In the UK the decline in smoking prevalence appears to be more a result of people giving up smoking rather than fewer people taking up the habit.[29]

Furthermore, Males[30] has concluded, from analysing the US statistics for a variety of youth 'problem' behaviours, that young people appear to respond more positively to measures aimed at reducing problem behaviour by both youth and adults than to measures aimed at preventing certain behaviour by youth alone.

All this was understood by the tobacco industry as long ago as 1953, as Sir Richard Doll has pointed out:[31]

> It was quite clear to me from then on that the (tobacco) industry knew that as long as young adults were smoking, and provided role models for children, it didn't matter how much you tried to educate children not to smoke, because they would not take any notice.

Not surprisingly, RJ Reynolds and Philip Morris in the USA have run advertising campaigns ostensibly to warn children against smoking, on the grounds that 'smoking is an adult habit'. It is therefore likely that the most effective interventions against children's smoking, in the long run, are those which affect adult smoking habits. Some of these are, of course, already known to affect children, eg price increases.[32]

A recent review[33] identifies the following major influences on adult smoking prevalence:

— price increases on tobacco

— smoking advice from the general practitioner

— mass media and community-based campaigns

— general health publicity in the media

In the long term, permanent declines in children's smoking can only be achieved in the context of a comprehensive national programme aimed at all appropriate age groups. Only in this way will we remove the ultimate incentive for children to take up smoking—the presence of adults as role models.

With regard to protecting the fetus and child from the substantial effects of passive smoking (Chapters 1 and 2), it is self evident that adult smoking needs to be considerably reduced and controlled. Smoking cessation among other adults as well as parents is therefore seen as a primary objective of a smoking control programme for children.

Implement effective smoking policies

Children are more likely to smoke if there are lax school policies or teachers smoke at school (see also Chapter 5). Where teachers, especially the headteacher, smoke the prevalence of smoking among the children is higher than in schools where teachers do not smoke.[32] In Finland, Rimpela *et al*[35] found that there was a relationship between lower cigarette consumption by pupils and strict teacher control on school premises. In practice, it is extremely difficult to isolate the effect of the school environment from what is taught in the classroom. However, one comprehensive evaluation programme in Canada[36] has shown the importance of both these elements.

In the UK major obstacles still remain since up to 1 in 5 teachers smoke, and the vast majority of schools permit smoking in staff rooms.[37] Smoking policies in schools for both pupils and teachers vary greatly and there appears to be a lack of consistent reasoning behind them.[38] However, progress may accelerate as public opinion continues to change in favour of more restrictive measures generally. In the USA restrictions on smoking in school and college premises are associated with decreased smoking in adolescents.[39]

There should be far greater effort in developing and implementing effective smoking control policies within schools and youth clubs. Costs of implementation will be trivial, and probably limited to an initial subsidy for teachers requesting help with cessation. Impact will be limited by acceptability—although, ultimately, there is no reason why smoking should not be completely forbidden relatively soon on all education premises on a 24-hour basis.

Promote non-smoking in public places as the norm

Smoking is already banned or restricted in many workplaces and public places, eg major shopping centres, and public transport. Such bans obviously contribute to the development of a climate of opinion unfavourable to smoking[40] and reduce the visible influence of adult role models on children. However, restrictions in public places are probably less common in places frequented by youth, eg pubs and football grounds. The Department of the Environment has recently issued guidelines encouraging greater provision of No Smoking areas, but it is doubtful whether such exhortation will rapidly increase the number of such areas. Legislative and regulatory measures are needed, with particular attention to the workplace.

STRENGTHEN COMMUNITY ACTION

Table 3   **Strategies to strengthen community action**

▓ Mobilise support and concern from parents, voluntary groups, local and national opinion formers (eg through Action on Smoking and Health (ASH), Coronary Prevention Group, Parents against Tobacco);

▓ Use mass media appropriately; undertake local, regional and national campaigns which encourage participation;

▓ Optimise informal settings to reinforce and support action (eg in youth clubs, leisure centres);

▓ Encourage young people to participate actively in smoking control activities, eg through health 'clubs', competitions, Smokebusters.

Mobilise support from concerned adults

With the increasing opportunities for the general public to influence the activities of public services there is now greater scope for community action on smoking issues. For example, school governors, who include parents, can influence the school curriculum more directly. District and Family Health Service Authorities are also becoming more consumer conscious. Public transport is more customer orientated etc. The question of smoking and young people is becoming much more of a social issue than previously and this concern needs to be fostered. Organisations like ASH, Coronary Prevention Group, Parents against Tobacco and others have a key role to play at national and regional level. More local, informed voluntary organisations could also play a valuable role in heightening awareness of the problems, and engaging key policy makers and providers of services in debate. Smoking in public places, illegal sales to children, and local authority policies on cigarette advertising are issues that could be addressed more forcefully through citizen action.

Use the mass media appropriately

Over the last two decades, mass media approaches have been used extensively in North America and most European countries.[41,42] This has often resulted because of the political imperative to be seen to be responding to the problem. However results are disappointing.

Television is pre-eminent in the mass media among adolescents, and teenage magazines is a rapidly growing market. Many teenagers will spend at least as much time watching television, listening to radio and going to the cinema as in compulsory education during school years. The major advantage of mass campaigns lies in the rapidity with which they can reach their target audience. For example, the recent teenage smoking TV advertising by the Health Education Authority reached 95% of teenagers in all social classes within three months of its launch.[43] However, the cost was considerable.

Media campaigns have been used successfully to de-glamorise smoking, and reach young people who are less accessible through traditional approaches. However, there is very little evidence that expensive, one-off media campaigns have any independent impact on young people's smoking. The few studies that exist give conflicting results.[44,45] Although such campaigns are attractive to many policy-makers, in general they do not represent a good value-for-money investment compared to other approaches.

The mass media can be a useful component of a broader programme of action: raising awareness, developing a climate of opinion and encouraging individual and community participation. Initiatives such as *No Smoking Day* and *Quit and Win* competitions offer more potential than isolated advertising campaigns because they require contributions from public and private sector organisations, health and education professionals and the general public. The greater the level of participation, the greater the level of legitimisation and endorsement which are important factors in shaping attitudes and behaviours.

In a review of recent research, Nutbeam[46] recommends that mass media should be used in the following ways:

— presenting non-smoking as attractive and acceptable behaviour

— supporting smoking cessation and giving high status to ex-smokers

— concentrating on the prevention of regular smoking rather than discouraging experimentation

— using a wide range of communication channels in combination, including television, radio and print media, for reinforcement

— coordinating media campaigns with other smoking education programmes based on more personal contacts (eg school work)

— sustaining a campaign over a long period rather than a short-term 'blitz'

Optimise use of youth clubs and other informal networks

Although school provides an efficient way of providing health education, there are alternative ways of reaching young people on a one-to-one basis. Using youth clubs and other informal networks is important because young people who become regular smokers are frequently those who feel alienated from the school and academic achievement. Health education through schools is unlikely to be effective for those groups.[46] Unfortunately, there are relatively few educational programmes which have been specifically targeted at young people outside the school environment.[6] This is an area which requires more research and development.

In the UK, a 'Pacesetters' magazine for teenagers was developed by the Health Education Council and a 'Heart Guards' magazine by Heartbeat Wales. These approaches were very popular and copies of the literature were widely distributed. More recently, the Health Education Authority has jointly produced materials with the National Youth Bureau for distribution throughout the youth club network. In Scotland and Wales health information for teenagers has been included in special publications developed for all school leavers. The effectiveness of these approaches is difficult to evaluate in isolation from other activities. They are however likely to add further momentum to a non-smoking culture.

Encourage participation in health 'clubs'

A number of health authorities and other agencies have set up 'Smoke-busters' Clubs for children, following their initiation in 'Project Smoke-free' in Manchester in 1985 by the Health Education Council and North Western Regional Health Authority. While these vary widely in their scope and activities, they typically consist of a club for 10–14-year-olds, which provides its members with badges, newsletters, occasional outings, competitions and, in some cases, discounts in appropriate shops. For example projects like 'Smokebusters' (North Western Regional Health Authority) and 'Pulse' (Heartbeat Wales) have invited club members to participate in competitions and design posters. They have also encouraged even young children to develop awareness of the influence of adults and the tobacco industry on their own attitudes and behaviour.[47]

The clubs are very popular, sometimes attracting several thousand members, and so can be costly to service unless sponsorship or other sources of income can be found. However, it is very difficult to establish to what extent membership results in a decline in the prevalence of smoking by youth although favourable effects on parents have been reported in Wales. Their main value probably lies in the extent to which they provide a means for encouraging participation, attracting publicity, creating awareness amongst adults and highlighting the problem of illegal sales and tobacco advertising at a local level.

REORIENTATE HEALTH SERVICES

Table 4   **Strategies to reorientate health services**

▓ Strengthen the public advocacy role of health professionals and health
authorities (eg through National Association of Health Authorities and
Trusts, Directors of Public Health Medicine Reports);

▓ Monitor and publish levels of smoking amongst young people at District
level on a regular basis, and encourage schools to do the same; monitor
rates of smoking in pregnancy;

▓ Ensure health premises and health professionals set a good example for
non-smoking and encourage health workers who smoke to give up;

▓ Ensure that smoking prevention and cessation is an important part of the
work of all health care professionals in both hospital and community
settings and monitor performance; give special attention to children,
pregnant women and parents;

▓ Accept responsibility for local, district and regional leadership and
coordination of effective smoking control programmes and set up
accountability mechanisms.

Raise public awareness

Health professionals and health authorities have a unique opportunity
of highlighting the problems of teenage smoking and demanding action
from relevant decision makers. An important first step is to develop a
database on the levels of smoking and to monitor trends over time. Low
cost measurement tools through school surveys have been developed in
Wales[48] and reports are produced every two years on teenage smoking
prevalence by county. Publication of the findings offers an excellent
way of creating awareness through media coverage. The annual reports
of Directors of Public Health Medicine provide another opportunity of
keeping the problem of teenage smoking on the public agenda.

Health authorities can also make an important contribution by
encouraging schools to measure smoking prevalence regularly among
their own pupils. As Gillies *et al*[49] have shown in Trent Regional Health
Authority, the feeding back of results to schools can stimulate considerable interest, and may help to develop local ownership of the
school's own smoking prevention programme.

Chapter 1 highlighted the considerable health impact on the fetus
from smoking in pregnancy. Although these data are collected routinely
by the maternity services, statistics are seldom published. This needs to
be rectified urgently in order that progress can be monitored. There are
no national data on the prevalence of smoking in pregnancy.

Health professionals and health authorities also have considerable opportunities to influence local and national decision makers through professional organisations, and bodies like the National Association of Health Authorities and Trusts. Smoking prevention should be one of the highest priorities for their public advocacy work.

Set a good example

Surveys of smoking in hospitals have shown that the NHS does not always lead by example.[50] Whilst those services that come directly into contact with children may be vigilantly non-smoking, there are many parts of hospitals frequented by young people that have a lax attitude to smoking, eg general outpatients, waiting areas, cafeterias etc. It is important that the NHS is seen as a 'shop window' for health by adults but even more so by children. Thus, health authorities should implement effective smoking control policies for their staff and premises.

Health professionals also have a special responsibility to demonstrate by personal example. Indeed much good work can be undermined by the negative role models of health professionals who smoke because they are perceived to 'know better' on such matters by the general public. Whilst smoking rates amongst health workers are lower in the UK than other parts of Europe, it is still disturbing that an appreciable number of doctors and considerably more nurses still smoke. This cannot be considered compatible with the objectives of health care. Smoking cessation support needs to be provided by the NHS for the NHS.

Intervene at individual and community level

All health care professionals can have a part to play in smoking control, either directly with children and their families or through the adults with whom they will come into contact. In addition to preventive education, special help and encouragement can be offered to smokers to give up. There is an extensive literature on the effectiveness of health professionals in smoking cessation and the benefits that accrue. Particular emphasis needs to be placed on adult smokers as mentioned previously. However, doctors, school nurses, health visitors and pharmacists should help young people to give up smoking wherever possible.

School nurses could, for example, play a particular role in organising Stop Smoking groups in schools. However, too much weight should not be placed on the potential contribution of this option in the long term, since the development of smoking among teenagers is highly erratic.[51]

Over and above their more traditional roles, health professionals can support smoking control at a community level. For example, they can demand No Smoking areas in public places, report tobacconists who sell cigarettes illegally to children, and complain about cigarette advertising near schools etc. Smoking prevention and cessation work should be a legitimate and important part of every health care worker's duties and performance should be audited in the same way as other responsibilities.

Accept responsibility for leadership

Health organisations, whether they are at primary care, unit, district or regional level, should accept they have a unique responsibility to develop smoking prevention programmes for the populations they serve. A number of model policies and programmes have been developed by ASH and other organisations (eg Ref 52). However, all too often the NHS is remarkably silent on this matter and leaves others to act even though it has considerable resources and opportunities at its disposal. The NHS has the most to gain by reducing smoking-related disease and thereby releasing resources for less preventable conditions. Every level of the NHS should be held accountable for ensuring that effective steps are taken to combat teenage smoking.

BUILD HEALTHY PUBLIC POLICY

Table 5   **Strategies to build healthy public policy**

- **Legislate against all forms of tobacco promotion, eg advertising of all tobacco products, including arts and sports sponsorship by tobacco companies;**

- **Maintain a strong price disincentive on cigarettes for young people by regularly increasing the real price of tobacco products through taxation;**

- **Introduce a special tax on tobacco to finance smoking prevention and related health research as in other countries (eg Australia, California);**

- **Raise the legal age for the sale of tobacco to 18, vigilantly enforce legislation and stop access of children to vending machines;**

- **Improve health warnings on tobacco products so that they are tougher, more prominent and young people orientated; introduce plain pack design;**

- **End all national and European aid for the production, manufacture, promotion and export of tobacco products and encourage diversification out of tobacco;**

continue

Table 5   **Strategies to build healthy public policy** *(continued)*

▓ **Promote non-smoking and severely restrict smoking in public places, especially where young people and children congregate, through legislation and regulation;**

▓ **Ensure that the National Health Service, education authorities and the national health promotion agencies undertake effective education and control programmes through specific funding and accountability mechanisms;**

▓ **Ensure that special attention is given by HMI and other school inspectors to the provision and quality of smoking education in schools, and that the National Curriculum continues to offer effective opportunities;**

▓ **Establish a Ministerial action group on smoking and health to ensure all relevant Departments of government play their full part and work together;**

▓ **Ask the National Audit Office and Public Accounts Committee to carry out periodic reviews on the development and implementation of smoking control programmes across the UK.**

Ban tobacco advertising and sponsorship

Evidence has already been presented in Chapter 5 on the important influence that cigarette advertising and tobacco sponsorship has on consumption, particularly in young people. Previous reports of the Royal College of Physicians have called for much stronger controls in this area. Not only is the need for action more compelling now due to high rates of smoking amongst girls, but the evidence that legislation will contribute to prevention has also become much stronger. Now is the time to act decisively.

Voluntary agreements which restrict advertising have achieved little and research has exposed the wide range of ways in which the tobacco industry circumvent such agreements, for example through the sponsorship of sporting and other media events, and the marketing of other products such as clothes using cigarette brandnames.[53]

The only effective way of eliminating the influence of tobacco advertising and sponsorship is legislation to enforce a complete ban on advertising and all other forms of indirect brand marketing. Parliament needs to enact such legislation as a matter of great urgency if the threat of teenage smoking in the UK is to be counteracted. Without leadership from government, other organisations are unlikely to respond enthusiastically to the challenge.

Maintain a strong price disincentive

The European Commission study of tobacco use has indicated that price has an inverse relationship with sales and consumption among young adults.[54] In those countries where government taxation policy has increased the cost of tobacco, lower prevalence and consumption rates among young people can be observed.

The reasons for this appear to be that those starting smoking are particularly susceptible to price disincentives.[32] This is not so much the case for established smokers where price 'elasticity' is lower. Continuing to raise tax on cigarettes by more than the inflation figure is therefore an important strategy for combating teenage smoking. The UK should set an example in this area and not be influenced by European countries that have lower rates of taxation.

The experience of California and Australia on the use of earmarked taxes on tobacco to fund smoking prevention and health research clearly demonstrates a benefit in terms of enhanced programme activity. The measure also ensures that due attention is given to tobacco taxation at each Budget. Removal of tobacco from the Retail Price Index would also mean that apparent inflation figures were not erroneously elevated. Tobacco is not an essential commodity.

Enforce legislation on illegal sales

Although the sale of tobacco to children under 16 has been illegal since 1933, the law is widely evaded.[27] In Wales, 29% of smokers aged 11–12 years buy their cigarettes from newsagents, tobacconists and sweet shops, and 54% of smokers aged 13–14.[55] Worse, despite the publicity generated by the passage of recent legislation, there has been an increase in the perceived ease of purchasing cigarettes.[56] Although there are no studies on smoking prevalence which separately evaluate the effect of reducing sales to under-16-year-olds, it is reasonable to surmise that restricting supply will influence both experimentation and consumption in children. Influencing the supply side is a well tried strategy for other public health problems, eg alcohol, illegal drugs.

Available interventions include educational campaigns to inform shopkeepers, parents and children of the law.[57] Well publicised surveys on the extent of illegal sales may act as a deterrent. Educational programmes in California have been shown to reduce the frequency of illegal sales.[58]

The tobacco industry could cooperate by threatening to withhold supplies from any tobacconist convicted of illegal sales. So far, it has always refused[59]—not surprisingly perhaps for an industry so dependent on the five-sixths of smokers who take up the habit before the age of 16.

The police, trading standards departments of county councils, parent teacher associations, concerned community groups as well as health workers all have a part to play to ensure the law is obeyed. Restricting the availability of vending machines is another valuable strategy to stop children purchasing tobacco.

Stimulated very successfully by Parents against Tobacco, new legislation has recently been introduced to strengthen enforcement. However, if rapid progress does not occur in curbing illegal sales to children, the possibility of licensing tobacco outlets (as for alcohol) should be seriously considered. This mechanism would ensure that careful vetting of prospective outlets was undertaken with the powerful sanction of withdrawing the tobacco licence.

There is an illogicality in the legal ages for selling tobacco and alcohol to young people in the UK. Even the tobacco industry agrees that smoking should be an adult habit—in which case there should be no objection to raising the tobacco age to 18 years as for alcohol. The argument is compelling since the impact on health and costs attributable to smoking are considerably greater than those for alcohol misuse. This measure would considerably assist in enforcement since children in school uniform are almost certainly below the age of 18 years, and there would be a significant impact on the availability of tobacco to older children in the 5th and 6th forms at secondary school who have an important influence on younger children at school through role modelling (Chapter 4). Experimentation and initiation of smoking would be likely to decline. Raising the legal age for selling tobacco to 18 years is therefore another intervention strategy worth pursuing.

Improve health warnings and control pack design

Health warnings on tobacco products can provide an immediate reminder to smokers of the health hazards they are incurring. Improvements have been made in recent years to the size, content and authorship. Whilst long-term smokers are likely to be hardened to such messages, those experimenting or just beginning may be more susceptible. Even smokers prefer strong unequivocal warnings prominently displayed.[60] Most of these new recruits will be children. Further developments are needed to improve health warnings which are tougher, more prominent and young people orientated. This should be a subject of on-going review and modification.

An added difficulty in the smoking control field is that cigarette packets are developed as a form of costume apparel, reinforcing images presented through advertising and sponsorship. The design, shape, packsize and colour can make a packet of cigarettes look attractive in its own right, like fashion wear for other commodities. A plain pack design could well reduce the attractiveness of cigarettes to young people. Details should be restricted to brand name, emission data and health warning using a controlled type-face etc. A neutral colour should be used with no other marketing features. This measure should also be included in legislation.

Influence the tobacco industry

Sadly, government and European Community assistance has been provided to tobacco manufacturers and producers. Such economic aid has been far in excess of the funds spent on prevention. This is an illogical, immoral and nonsensical strategy and should be stopped forthwith. Those companies with tobacco interests should be positively encouraged to diversify out of tobacco. Economic policies should be developed to make the tobacco business increasingly unprofitable.

Regulations to reduce toxic emissions in tobacco products could both decrease health risks in certain situations and increase the ingredient cost and the complexity of manufacturing. The Department of Industry should demonstrate that they are actively supporting the health targets for smoking outlined for England in 'Health of the Nation'.[1]

Ensure national leadership and accountability

Governments are expected to lead—to act in the interests of the greater good—and to be ahead of public opinion. The control of teenage smoking is an area where such leadership is clearly necessary. The United Kingdom's record on smoking in children is not good; rates have hardly changed over the last decade and the very worrying feature of epidemic levels of smoking by girls has now emerged.

Restrictions on smoking in public places is an important contribution to stopping young people smoke (see p. 61) and there is much that the Department of Environment can do to encourage this. The health and education services also have a vital part to play. The Departments of Health and Education both have a responsibility to ensure that all those agencies and authorities responsible to them address smoking control as the major public health priority over the next decade. The same applies to the national health promotional/health education bodies in England, Northern Ireland, Scotland and Wales. Specific funding and accountability mechanisms are needed to ensure that this occurs.

The case for improved education about smoking in schools is compelling. The Education Reform Act 1988 specifies that a balanced and broadly based curriculum should be provided which

> promotes the spiritual, moral, cultural, mental and physical development of pupils at the school and of society; and prepares such pupils for the opportunities, responsibilities and experiences of adult life.

The evidence in previous chapters demonstrates that children are ill-equipped to resist the pressure to smoke. Further developments in the National Curriculum in schools could give greater prominence to health education with special reference to smoking, and to aid this process health sciences should be an examinable subject area for which results are published. HMI and the new arrangement for school inspection and advisory teachers have clear opportunities to ensure progress is made. The Department of Education should give a lead.

The need for inter-Departmental action within government has been emphasised in this report, as it has in previous College documents. The Government should develop a comprehensive set of policies to combat smoking.[61] The Departments of Health, Education, Environment, Trade and Industry, the Treasury and the Territorial Departments for Northern Ireland, Scotland and Wales all have a unique and vital role to play. Smoking control strategies should therefore be a Cabinet responsibility and a Ministerial Action Group is needed to coordinate responses. If groups have been established for alcohol, drugs and AIDS then surely the case for a group for smoking is overwhelming given the scale of the problem and the costs incurred.

Government itself has to be accountable for its actions. There is a role here for the National Audit Office and the Public Accounts Committee which are increasingly becoming concerned with health issues and effective health expenditure. There is no other health issue in the UK which offers a better return on investment than the control of smoking. Periodic reviews and scrutinies should be established to call to task government and other public bodies in an area which is so vital to Britain's social and economic development.

SUMMARY AND CONCLUSIONS

Health promoting schools

Schools have an important role to play in developing the necessary personal and social skills to help teenagers resist smoking; and in helping some parents to give up. The delay in recruitment will however, by itself, only make a small contribution to reductions in smoking prevalence, and this may not be long term. The benefits of a favourable education curriculum can be enhanced in 'health promoting schools' — where lesson content is supported by other initiatives, eg forbidding smoking on the premises and community action to reduce illegal sales and advertising outside schools. The NHS has a useful role to play in supporting schools to maximise their contribution. The effects of more exotic interventions, such as advertising campaigns aimed solely at youth and 'Smokebusters' Clubs, are uncertain. Both require substantial financial investment for full implementation. Much research and development is still needed concerning the forms of direct action with children that are most effective.

Comprehensive action

In the long run, however, children's smoking cannot be reduced significantly below its present level except as part of a comprehensive strategy to reduce smoking in the community generally. Every adult who smokes in front of a child is, in a small way, teaching that child to smoke. Smoking is contagious. It needs to be regarded as if it were an infectious disease which passes by imitation from person to person and from generation to generation. The increasing problem of girls' smoking is particularly worrying.

Government leadership

In the context of the national strategy for England[1] and similar developments in Northern Ireland, Scotland and Wales,[2,3,62] it is recommended that the government should immediately initiate a major long-term programme to reduce smoking prevalence in all age groups. This should involve action by all available means, but with major emphasis on legislation, fiscal policy and community-based campaigns to help adults to give up, and increased activity within the health services. Tables 1–5 have summarised the sorts of intervention that could be beneficial.

Health promotion campaigning

To help bring these about, the NHS and all other health promoting agencies, both voluntary and statutory, should support health ministers both with advocacy and active efforts to publicise the magnitude of the current epidemic of smoking-related disease. It is no coincidence that the most rapid recent declines in prevalence abroad have occurred wherever vigorous public campaigning has been combined with increased restrictions on advertising, real price increases, mass media education and health service-based cessation campaigns — as in Canada,[63] California[64] and New Zealand.[65]

Legislation and monitoring

A legislative framework to support these strategies is vital. We require good, wide-ranging and localised baseline data, top-level inter-disciplinary advisory groups to guide the formation and implementation of the necessary legislation; and a strong 'watchdog' body to monitor effects of the legislation and to counteract industry attempts to sabotage it. Most important of all, tobacco control policy should be agreed by the government as a whole, at Cabinet level, to ensure that the Department of Health is supported by other Departments.

The future

The failure by successive governments to take the necessary steps, despite countless requests from those concerned for the nation's health, has allowed the continued recruitment of new smokers. This is at a rate which will ensure that tobacco smoking continues to be the nation's largest preventable cause of illness, disability and premature death for many decades to come. As we have said in previous reports, effective action against tobacco could achieve a greater reduction in mortality and morbidity among future generations than any other single measure known to us. Future generations may well ask why it took over a quarter of a century for the government to take the necessary action.

We should be more ambitious than the government's target for a one-third reduction in adult smoking prevalence by the year 2000. We should look longer term to the 50th anniversary of the first College report in the year 2012. We should expect to mark that year with the announcement from the final OPCS prevalence survey that teenage smoking has now fallen to statistically insignificant levels. We can then, at last, begin to celebrate our children's freedom from the greatest national epidemic of our time.

Major Findings

Smoking, the fetus and early life

1. Spontaneous abortions (miscarriages) of viable fetuses are increased in pregnant smokers by more than one-quarter.

2. Premature labour is twice as common in pregnant smokers.

3. Babies born to mothers who smoke are lighter by an average 200 grams (approximately half a pound). Paternal smoking also makes babies significantly lighter.

4. Stillbirths and early neonatal deaths (perinatal mortality) are increased by approximately one-third in babies of smokers.

5. The effects of smoking in pregnancy extend well beyond infancy with a reduction in growth and educational achievement.

The effects of passive smoking on the health of children

6. Children of smoking parents inhale the same amount of nicotine as if they themselves smoked 60–150 cigarettes per year.

7. Over one-quarter of the risk of death due to the sudden infant death syndrome (cot death) is attributable to maternal smoking (equivalent to one death per day in England and Wales).

8. Infants of parents who smoke are twice as likely to suffer from serious respiratory infection.

9. Symptoms of asthma are twice as common in the children of smokers.

10. One-third of cases of 'glue ear', the commonest cause of deafness in children, is attributable to parental smoking.

11. Children of parents who smoke more than 10 cigarettes per day are shorter than children of non-smokers.

12. Passive smoking in childhood is an important cause of school absenteeism accounting for one in seven days lost.

13. Parental smoking is responsible for at least 17,000 admissions to hospital each year of children under the age of five.

14. Passive smoking during childhood predisposes children to developing chronic obstructive airway disease and cancer as adults.

15. Elimination of parental smoking during early childhood would result in a substantial reduction in infant mortality.

Health problems of children who smoke

16. Nicotine is a drug of addiction. Many young smokers are addicted to nicotine and develop withdrawal symptoms on stopping.

17. Smoking is an important marker for other types of drug abuse, eg alcohol, cannabis, cocaine etc.

18. Young smokers have more respiratory infections with more time off work and school.

19. Teenage smokers have between two and six times more cough and sputum than non-smokers.

20. Asthmatics who smoke have worse symptoms and lung function than non-smoking asthmatics.

21. The earlier children start smoking, the greater the risk of lung cancer in later life.

22. Smoking is a cardiac stimulant, which magnifies the effect of stress on the heart.

23. Smokers are less physically fit being both slower at sprints and endurance running. The performance in a half-marathon of a smoker of 20 cigarettes per day is that of a non-smoker 12 years older.

24. Smoking increases blood coagulability and adversely affects blood lipids.

25. Subarachnoid brain haemorrhage is six times more common in young smokers than non-smokers.

26. The earlier children start smoking, the younger they develop heart disease.

27. Smoking increases skin ageing and wrinkling.

28. Female smokers are two to three times more likely to be infertile.

29. Smoking affects immunity and has been associated with an increased risk of HIV infection.

Prevalence of smoking in the young

30. Every day in Great Britain 450 children start smoking.

31. One-quarter of UK school leavers aged 15 years smoke regularly, ie at a time when it is illegal to sell them cigarettes. Little change has occurred in the last decade in the proportion of children who smoke. Present data suggest more girls than boys now smoke.

32. By the age of 11 years, one-third of children, and by 16 years, two-thirds of children have experimented with smoking.

33. Most adult smokers had started regular smoking before the age of 18.

34. The high prevalence of regular smoking in young people and the lack of any significant decline in the last decade is alarming.

Factors that encourage children to smoke

35. Smoking in the young is directly related to adult smoking. Important reductions in children's smoking will occur only when the role modelling of adults is considerably reduced.

36. Young regular smokers tend to be rebellious with poor self-image and indulge in risk-taking behaviour.

37. Parental smoking and attitudes are critically important influences on whether a child will smoke. Children are seven times less likely to smoke if they perceive strong disapproval from their parents.

38. In older children, the smoking habits of friends are important. Going against the group norm is difficult and refusal skills have to be learnt.

39. Non-smoking teachers and strict school No Smoking policies reduce cigarette consumption both in and out of school and in later life.

40. There are one-quarter of a million retail outlets selling tobacco in the UK of which half break the law on sales to children.

41. Regular price increases through taxation reduce tobacco consumption whilst government tax revenue actually increases.

42. The tobacco industry spends at least £72 million per year in the UK advertising and promoting cigarettes. Tobacco advertising perpetuates the myth that tobacco has significant positive qualities of success, glamour, speed and adult behaviour.

43. A tobacco price increase results in a greater reduction in consumption in young people than in adults. In terms of average disposable income, the price of a pack of cigarettes has halved in the last 30 years.

Measures to reduce smoking in the young

44. Children are considerably influenced by tobacco advertising and promotion, particularly girls. They need to be taught the skills to resist the marketing pressures to smoke.

45. There is an urgent need for immediate action to prevent an epidemic of smoking related disease in women occurring as a result of girls starting to smoke during school years.

46. A range of intervention strategies are available which if developed and implemented comprehensively would have a major effect in reducing children's smoking to undetectable levels.

47. These strategies should comprise developing personal skills in young people, creating supportive environments, strengthening community action, reorientating health services and building healthy public policy.

48. A ban on tobacco advertising and sponsorship as part of a comprehensive Tobacco Act would have a significant impact on the uptake of tobacco by young people in the UK.

49. There is an urgent need to develop coherent UK government and European Community strategies and policies on tobacco control if the public's health is to be substantially improved.

Recommendations

The whole of society carries a responsibility for the health of its children. As well as every individual setting an example to children by not smoking, the following groups have particular responsibilities and opportunities in respect of smoking to act in the interest of children's health.

1. PARENTS should:

▪ Stop smoking before and during pregnancy because this may harm their baby

▪ Seek advice, counselling and support to stop smoking in pregnancy and afterwards

▪ Refrain from smoking after pregnancy because smoking may damage their children's health and make it more likely that their children will smoke

▪ Give a firm message of disapproval of smoking to their children

▪ Support non-smoking education programmes in school and in the community

▪ Encourage schools, education authorities, governing bodies, health authorities and councils to face up to their responsibility to safeguard children's health

▪ Report breaches in the tobacco control measures for children, eg illegal sales and advertising.

2. SCHOOL AND EDUCATION AUTHORITIES should:

▪ Use innovative teaching methods to help young people develop the skills to resist peer and social pressures to smoke both in primary and secondary school

▪ Involve the family and parents in non-smoking education to reinforce classroom teaching

▪ Provide relevant information on short- and long-term effects of smoking on fitness, health, personal expenditure, appearance, environment, the economy and society as a whole

▪ Offer help to teachers to stop smoking

▪ Improve training of teachers and youth workers in health education

- Implement a total No Smoking policy in all schools, colleges and youth clubs

- Encourage the participation of children and young people in smoke-free programmes at school and in the community.

3. THE MEDIA should:

- Recognise and accept their responsibility towards safeguarding the health of children

- Understand that promotion of tobacco and role models who smoke increase uptake in children

- Refuse to accept overt or covert tobacco advertising and sponsorship

- Take action which encourages children not to smoke and avoid inadvertent editorial promotion of smoking

- Support smoking education programmes and give high status to non-smokers and ex-smokers.

4. THE NATIONAL HEALTH SERVICE should:

- Accept responsibility for local, district and regional leadership, co-ordinate effective smoking control programmes, and set up accountability mechanisms

- Monitor and publish levels of smoking amongst young people at district level on a regular basis and encourage schools to do the same

- Monitor prevalence of smoking in pregnancy

- Ensure that smoking prevention and cessation is an important part of the work of all health care professionals in both hospital and community settings, and monitor their performance. Give special attention to children, pregnant women and parents

- Ensure all health premises are designated non-smoking and that health professionals set a good example by not smoking

- Encourage health workers who smoke to give up and provide smoking cessation opportunities for them

- Strengthen their public advocacy role for a smoke-free society, for example through the National Association of Health Authorities and Trusts, and through reports of Directors of public health medicine reports.

5. LOCAL GOVERNMENT should:

- Agree a No-Smoking policy for the council and ban smoking at council meetings

- Use all its powers to prevent tobacco advertising and promotion in the community

- Encourage Trading Standards Officers (a) to enforce legislation on sales of cigarettes to children and actively prosecute offenders, and (b) to monitor and take action on breaches of advertising controls

- Enable environmental health officers to encourage non-smoking policies in public places, work sites etc.

- Ban all smoking in leisure and sports centres and other public places owned by the council, especially where young people congregate

- Implement effective smoking control policies for their own employees and offer them help with smoking cessation.

6. TOBACCO RETAILERS AND RETAIL ORGANISATIONS should:

- Ensure that they do not endanger the health of children by selling or by permitting the sale of cigarettes to them

- Prominently display notices indicating that the sale of cigarettes to underage children is prohibited.

7. HEALTH PROMOTION AGENCIES should:

- Ensure that accessible and relevant information on all aspects of smoking is available to children, parents, schools, education authorities, health authorities etc.

- Mount and evaluate community-based initiatives for young people and adults, eg Smokebusters, Quit-and-Win Contests

- Encourage citizen action in relation to smoking in public places, work sites etc to create a climate of opinion which promotes non-smoking as the norm

- Mobilise public opinion to influence local and national decision-makers

- Use the media on a planned and opportunistic basis to promote a smoke-free society

- Recognise their responsibility to the health of young people when planning and setting priorities.

- Continue to invest in research and development studies and experimental and demonstration projects.

8. CENTRAL GOVERNMENT should:

- Legislate to ban all forms of direct and indirect tobacco promotion and advertising including arts and sports sponsorship

■ Maintain a strong price disincentive on cigarettes for young people by regularly increasing the real price of tobacco products through taxation

■ Introduce a special tax on tobacco to finance smoking prevention and related health research

■ Raise the legal age for buying tobacco to 18 years

■ Diligently enforce and monitor legislation on sales to children and, if current measures are ineffective, consider introducing licensing arrangements for the sale of tobacco

■ Improve health warnings on tobacco products so they are tougher, more prominent and oriented to young people

■ Introduce plain packaging requirements for cigarette manufacturers

■ End all national and European aid for production, manufacture and promotion of tobacco products and encourage diversification out of tobacco

■ Enact legislation to ban smoking within 5 years in public places and especially in all schools, sports and leisure facilities and NHS premises

■ Enact legislation for the right to work in a smoke-free environment

■ Establish a Ministerial Action Group to ensure that relevant Departments develop and implement effective tobacco control policies.

9. DOCTORS should:

■ Set an example by not smoking in public, and seek help to give up

■ Demonstrate concern for effective smoking control policies in their own workplaces

■ Offer sympathetic and effective smoking cessation advice to their parents and encourage non-smokers including children to remain smoke-free

■ Challenge publicly poor role models in public life and irresponsible organisations

■ Write to Members of Parliament and to local counsellors to inform them of smoking and health issues

■ Support and encourage medical and other health bodies who are working at a national level to combat smoking

■ Initiate a 'Doctors' Smoke-Free Action Group' to ensure progress is made locally.

APPENDIX 1

(a) Estimate of smoking-related spontaneous abortions; England and Wales 1991

Number of live births = 688,000

Assuming that
  (i) proportion of pregnancies that end in spontaneous abortion in relation to live births is 10% (ie 68,800 per year)
 (ii) spontaneous abortion increased by 27% in smokers (see Chapter 1)
(iii) 25% of mothers actively smoke through pregnancy (see Chapter 1).

Population attributable risk = 6.3%
ie 4,300 spontaneous abortions per year attributable to maternal smoking.

(b) Estimate of smoking-related perinatal deaths; England and Wales 1991

Number of live births = 688,000

Assuming that
  (i) perinatal mortality = 8.1/1000 live births (ie 5,573 perinatal deaths per year)
 (ii) perinatal mortality is increased by 33% in maternal smokers (see Chapter 1)
(iii) 25% of mothers actively smoke through pregnancy (see Chapter 1).

Population attributable risk = 7.6%
ie 420 perinatal deaths attributable to maternal smoking.

APPENDIX 2

Methodology for calculating the number of hospital admissions in children under five attributable to maternal smoking

The percentage of hospital admissions attributable to maternal smoking (population attributable risk %) is given by:

$$PAR\% = \frac{P_1R_1 + P_2R_2 + P_3R_3 - (P_1 + P_2 + P_3)}{P_1R_1 + P_2R_2 + P_3R_3 + [1 - (P_1 + P_2 + P_3)]} \times 100$$

where:

PAR = Population attributable risk %

R = Relative risk of admission in exposed children compared to non-exposed

P = Proportion of children exposed.

Adjusted relative risks for hospital admission in UK children exposed to varying degrees of maternal smoking are available from the 1970 birth cohort study [Ch 2 Ref 53]; this gives relative risks of:

1.1   for mothers smoking 1–9 cigarettes a day (R_1)
1.2   for mothers smoking 10–19 cigarettes a day (R_2)
1.3   for mothers smoking 20+ cigarettes a day (R_3)

This study also measured the proportion of children exposed to different levels of maternal smoking, but the prevalence of smoking has declined since the 1970s. Current exposure data are not available at national level but a reasonable estimate can be made from local studies and from knowledge of smoking rates in the relevant female age group. For the purposes of this calculation the following exposure estimates have been used:

10% of children exposed to 0–9 cigarettes a day (P_1)
10% of children exposed to 10–19 cigarettes a day (P_2)
10% of children exposed to 20+ cigarettes a day (P_3)

This gives:

$$PAR\% = \frac{(1.1 + 1.2 + 1.3)0.1 - 0.3}{(1.1 + 1.2 + 1.3)0.1 + 0.7} \times 100$$

$$= \frac{0.06}{1.06} \times 100$$

$$= 5.70\%$$

Thus 5.70% of all admissions to hospital in children under 5 years can be attributed to maternal smoking.

The number of hospital admissions made by under fives can be estimated from the 0–4-year-old population in the UK (3.38 million in 1991) and the proportion of 0–4-year-olds found to have been admitted to hospital in the previous year in the General Household Survey 1988 [Ch 2 Ref 58]; this gives a figure of 304,200.

The annual number of hospital admissions in children under 5 years attributable to passive smoking is therefore 17,219.

APPENDIX 3

Methodology estimating the proportion of school absenteeism attributable to maternal smoking

Information on the relative risk of school absenteeism in children exposed to maternal smoking has been researched in a study undertaken in 1987 in Tyne and Wear and Cumbria [Ch 2 Ref 54].

This study provides the following information:

Adjusted relative risk of absenteeism
in children of mothers who smoke (R) = 1.39

(adjusted for children's personal smoking
habits and catchment area of school)

Proportion of children exposed to maternal
smoking (P) = 40%

The population attributable risk % can be then calculated as follows:

$$\frac{P \times R - P}{P \times R + (1 - P)} \times 100$$

$$= \frac{0.4 \times 1.39 - 0.4}{0.4 \times 1.39 + (1-0.4)} \times 100$$

$$= 13.5\%$$

APPENDIX 4
Model tobacco control policy

The essentials of a tobacco control policy, which could be applied internationally are:

1. Prohibiting all forms of tobacco promotion.

2. Regular rises in the real price of tobacco products, via taxation.

3. Increased public education and public health information programmes.

4. Tougher and more prominent health warnings on packs; introduce plain package design.

5. Making non-smoking the norm in all public places, with designated smoking areas where appropriate.

6. Stopping sales to children.

7. Reducing emission levels of toxic components.

8. Ending incentives for tobacco production and manufacture; and encouraging diversification by those dependent on tobacco.

References

Preface

1. Royal College of Physicians. *Smoking and health*. A report on smoking in relation to lung cancer and other diseases. London: Pitman Medical 1962.
2. Royal College of Physicians. *Smoking and health now*. A new report on smoking and its effects on health. London: Pitman Medical 1971.
3. Royal College of Physicians. *Smoking or health*. London: Pitman Medical 1977.
4. Royal College of Physicians. *Health or smoking*. A follow-up report. London: Pitman Medical 1983.
5. Wald NW, Booth C, Doll R *et al* (eds). *Passive smoking: a health hazard*. London: Imperial Cancer Research Fund and Cancer Research Campaign 1991.
6. Department of Health. *The health of the nation*. A consultative document for health in England. Cm1523. London: HMSO 1991.

Note: References 1–3 are out of print. Reference 4 can be obtained from the Royal College of Physicians.

Chapter 1: **Passive smoking and the health of the fetus**

1. Simpson WJ. A preliminary report of cigarette smoking and the incidence of prematurity. *Am J Obstet Gynecol* 1957; **73**: 808–15.
2. Madeley RJ, Gillies PA, Power FL, Symonds EM. Nottingham Mothers Stop Smoking Project—baseline survey of smoking in pregnancy. *Community Med* 1989; **11**: 124–30.
3. Gillies PA, Madeley RJ, Power FL. Why do pregnant women smoke? *Public Health* 1989; **103**: 337–43.
4. Donovan JW. Randomised controlled trial of anti-smoking advice in pregnancy. *Br J Prev Soc Med* 1977; **31**: 6–12.
5. McKnight A, Merrett JD. Smoking in pregnancy—a health education problem. *J R Coll Gen Pract* 1986; **36**: 161–4.
6. Eiser C, Eiser JR. Health education needs of primigravidae. *Child Care Health and Development* 1985; **11**: 53–60.
7. Lilley J, Forster DP. A randomised controlled trial of individual counselling of smokers in pregnancy. *Public Health* 1986; **100**: 309–15.
8. Gillies PA, Madeley RJ, Power FL. Smoking cessation in pregnancy—a controlled trial of the impact of new technology and friendly encouragement. In: Aski, Hisanichi and Tominaga (eds). *Smoking and health 1987*. Amsterdam: Elsevier Science Publications 1988.
9. Lowe CR. Effect of mothers' smoking habits on birth weight of their children. *Br Med J* 1959; **4**: 673–6.
10. Stein Z, Kline J. Smoking, alcohol and reproduction. *Am J Public Health* 1983; **73**: 1154–6.
11. Mitchell MC, Lerner E. A comparison of pregnancy outcome in overweight and normal weight women. *J Am Coll Nutr* 1989; **8**: 617–24.

12. Tenovuo AH, Kero PA, Korvenranta HJ *et al*. Risk factors associated with severely small for gestational age neonates. *Am J Perinatol* 1988; **5**: 267–71.
13. Olsen J, Pereira A-da-C, Olsen SF. Does maternal tobacco smoking modify the effect of alcohol on fetal growth? *Am J Public Health* 1991; **81**: 69–73.
14. Meyer M, Jonas B, Tonascia J. Perinatal events associated with maternal smoking. *Am J Epidemiol* 1976; **103**: 464–76.
15. Haddow JE, Knight GJ, Palomaki GE, Kloza BM, Wald NJ. Cigarette consumption and serum cotinine in relation to birth weight. *Br J Obstet Gynaecol* 1987; **94**: 678–81.
16. Mathai M, Skinner A, Lawton K, Weindling AM. Maternal smoking, urinary cotinine level and birth weight. *Aust NZ J Obstet Gynaecol* 1990; **30**: 33–6.
17. Sexton M, Hebel JR. A clinical trial of change in maternal smoking and its effect on birth weight. *J Am Med Assoc* 1984; **251**: 911–5.
18. MacArthur C, Knox EG. Smoking in pregnancy: effects of stopping at different stages. *Br J Obstet Gynaecol* 1988; **95**: 551–5.
19. Hebel JR, Fox NL, Sexton M. Dose response of birth weight to various measures of maternal smoking during pregnancy. *J Clin Epidemiol* 1988; **41**: 483–9.
20. Butler NR, Goldstein H, Ross EM. Cigarette smoking in pregnancy: its influence on birth weight and perinatal mortality. *Br Med J* 1972; **2**: 127–30.
21. Yerushalmy S. The relationship of parents' cigarette smoking to outcome of pregnancy: implications as to the problem of inferring causation from observed association. *Am J Epidemiol* 1972; **93**: 443–56.
22. Butler NR, Alberman ED (eds). *Perinatal problems*. The Second Report of the 1958 British Perinatal Mortality Survey. Edinburgh and London: Livingstone 1969.
23. Frazier TM, Davis CH, Goldstein H, Goldberg ID. Cigarette smoke and prematurity: a prospective study. *Am J Obstet Gynecol* 1961; **81**: 988–96.
24. Underwood PB, Kesler KF, O'Lane JM, Collagan DA. Parental smoking empirically related to pregnancy outcome. *Obstet Gynecol* 1967; **29**: 1–8.
25. Brooke OG, Anderson HR, Bland JM, Peacock JL, Stewart C. Effect on birth weight of smoking, alcohol, caffeine, socio-economic factors and psychosocial stress. *Br Med J* 1989; **298**: 795–801.
26. Abell TD, Baker LC, Ramsey CN. The effects of maternal smoking on infant birth weight. *Fam Med* 1991; **23**: 103–7.
27. Fung KP, Wong TW, Lau SP. Ethnic determinants of perinatal statistics of Chinese: demography of China, Hong Kong and Singapore. *Int J Epidemiol* 1989; **18**: 127–31.
28. D'Souza SW, Black P, Richards B. Smoking in pregnancy: association with skinfold thickness, maternal weight gain and fetal size at birth. *Br Med J* 1981; **282**: 1661–3.
29. Elwood PC, Sweetnam PM, Gray OP, Davies DP, Wood PD. Growth of children from 0–5 years: with special reference to mothers smoking in pregnancy. *Ann Hum Biol* 1987; **14**: 543–57.
30. Tenovuo A, Kero P, Piekhala P, Korvenranta H, Sillanpaa M, Erkkola R. Growth of 519, small for gestational age, infants during the first two years of life. *Acta Paediatr Scand* 1987; **76**: 636–46.

31. Goldstein H. Factors influencing the height of seven-year-old children. *Hum Biol* 1971; **43**: 92–111.
32. Fogelman KR, Manor O. Smoking in pregnancy and development into early adulthood. *Br Med J* 1988; **297**: 1233–6.
33. Rantakallio P. Groups at risk. In: Low birth weight infants and perinatal mortality. *Acta Paediatr Scand* 1969 (suppl); **193**: 1–71.
34. Himmelberger D, Brown B, Cohen F. Cigarette smoking during pregnancy and the occurrence of spontaneous abortion and congenital abnormality. *Am J Epidemiol* 1978; **108**: 470–9.
35. Harlap S, Shiono P. Alcohol, smoking and incidence of spontaneous abortion in first and second trimester. *Lancet* 1980; **ii**: 173–6.
36. Werler MM, Pober B, Holmes LB. Smoking and pregnancy. *Teratology* 1985; **32**: 473–81.
37. Naeye RL. Abruptis placentae and placenta previa: frequency, perinatal mortality and cigarette smoking. *Obstet Gynecol* 1980; **55**: 701–4.
38. Voigt LK, Hollonbach KA, Krohn MA, Daling JR, Hickok DE. The relationship of abruptis placentae with maternal smoking and small for gestational age infants. *Obstet Gynecol* 1990; **75**: 771–4.
39. Hubner F, Schonlau H, Stumpf C. Der Einfluss von risikofaktoren auf die Fruhgeburtlichkeit und auf das kindliche Behinden nach der Geburt. *Geburtshilfe Perinatol* 1988; **192**: 91–5.
40. Wen SW, Goldenberg RL, Cutler GR, Hoffman HJ, Oliver SP, Davis RO, DuBard MB. Smoking, maternal age, fetal growth and gestational age at delivery. *Am J Obstet Gynecol* 1990; **162**: 53–8.
41. Rush D, Andrews J, Kristal A. Maternal cigarette smoking during pregnancy, adiposity, social class and perinatal outcome in Cardiff, Wales, 1965–77. *Am J Perinatol* 1990; **7**: 319–26.
42. Malloy MH, Kleinman JC, Land GH, Schrann WF. The association of maternal smoking with age and cause of infant death. *Am J Epidemiol* 1988; **128**: 46–55.
43. Comstock GW, Shah FK, Meyer MB, Abby H. Low birth weight and neonatal mortality rate related to maternal smoking and socio-economic status. *Am J Obstet Gynecol* 1971; **111**: 53–9.
44. Haddow JR, Knight GJ, Palomaki GE, Haddow PK. Estimating fetal morbidity and mortality resulting from cigarette smoke exposure measuring cotinine levels in maternal serum. *Transplacental effects on fetal health.* New York: Alan R. Liss Inc 1988; 289–300.
45. Villar J, De Onis M, Kestler E, Bolanos F, Cerezo R, Bernedes H. The differential neonatal morbidity of the intrauterine growth retardation syndrome. *Am J Obstet Gynecol* 1990; **163**: 151–7.
46. Garn JM, Petzold AS, Ridella SA, Johnston M. Effect of smoking during pregnancy on Apgar and Bayley scores. *Lancet* 1980; **ii**: 912–3.
47. Hill LM, Kleinberg F. Effects of drugs and chemicals on the fetus and the newborn. *Mayo Clin Proc* 1985; **59**: 755–6.
48. Teasdale F, Ghislaine JJ. Morphological changes in the placentas of smoking mothers: a histomorphometric study. *Biol Neonate* 1989; **55**: 251–9.
49. Dadak C, Kefalides A, Sinzinger H, Weber F. Reduced umbilic-artery prostacyclin formation in complicated pregnancies. *Am J Obstet Gynecol* 1982; **144**: 792–5.
50. Kuhbert BR, Kuhbert BN, Zarlingo TJ. Associations between placental

cadmium and zinc and parity in pregnant women who smoke. *Obstet Gynecol* 1988; **71**: 67–70.

51. Metcalf J, Costiloe P, Crosby WM, Sandstead H, Milne D. Smoking in pregnancy: relation of birth weight to maternal plasma carotene and cholesterol levels. *Obstet Gynecol* 1989; **74**: 302–9.

52. Everson R, Randerath E, Santella RM, Avitts TA, Weinstein IB, Randerath K. Quantitative associations between DNA damage in human placenta and maternal smoking and birth weight. *J Natl Cancer Inst* 1988; **80**: 567–76.

53. *Committee to study the prevention of low birth weight*. Washington DC: National Academy Press 1988; 41.

54. Magnusson CGM. Maternal smoking influences cord serum IgE levels and increases the risk for subsequent infant allergy. *J Allergy Clin Immunol* 1986; **78**: 898–904.

55. Rantakallio P. Relationship of maternal smoking to morbidity and mortality of the child up to age five. *Acta Paediatr Scand* 1978; **67**: 621–31.

56. Harlap S, Davies AM. Infant admissions to hospital and maternal smoking. *Lancet* 1974; **i**: 529–32.

57. Taylor B, Wadsworth J. Maternal smoking during pregnancy and lower respiratory tract illness in early life. *Arch Dis Child* 1987; **66**: 786–91.

58. Tager IB, Weiss ST, Munoz A, Rosner B, Speizer FE. Longitudinal study of the effects of maternal smoking on pulmonary function in children. *N Engl J Med* 1983; **309**: 699–703.

59. Hasselbad V, Humble CG, Graham MG, Anderson HS. Indoor environmental determinants of lung function. *Am Rev Respir Dis* 1981; **123**: 479–85.

60. Bulterys MG, Greenland S, Kraus JK. Chronic fetal hypoxia and sudden infant death syndrome: interaction between maternal smoking and low hematocrit during pregnancy. *Pediatrics* 1990; **86**: 535–40.

61. Haglund B, Cnattingius S. Cigarette smoking as a risk factor for sudden infant death syndrome: a population based study. *Am J Public Health* 1990; **80**: 29–32.

62. Goldings J, Paterson M, Kinlen LJ. Factors associated with child cancer in a national cohort study. *Br J Cancer* 1990; **62**: 304–8.

63. Neutel CI, Buck C. Effect of smoking during pregnancy on the risk of cancer in children. *J Natl Cancer Inst* 1971; **47**: 59–63.

64. Yerushalmy J. Statistical considerations and evaluation of epidemiological evidence. In: James G (ed). *Tobacco and health*. Springfield, Illinois: C.C. Thomas 1962.

65. MacMahon B, Alpert M, Salber EJ. Infant weight and parental smoking habits. *Am J Epidemiol* 1965; **82**: 247–61.

66. Rubin DH, Kraslinikoff PA, Leventhal JM, Weile W, Berget A. Effect of passive smoking on birth weight. *Lancet* 1986; **ii**: 415–7.

67. Martin TR, Bracken MB. Association of low birth weight with passive smoking exposure in pregnancy. *Am J Epidemiol* 1986; **124**: 633–42.

68. Vine MF, Hulka BS, Everson RB *et al. Cotinine levels in blood, urine and semen of smokers and non-smokers*. Presented at the 2nd Annual Meeting of the International Society for Environmental Epidemiology, 1990.

69. Davis DL. Paternal smoking and fetal health. *Lancet* 1991; **337**: 123.

70. Wainwright RL. Change in observed birthweight associated with change in maternal cigarette smoking. *Am J Epidemiol* 1983; **117**: 668–75.

71. Gillies PA. Anti-smoking intervention in pregnancy—impact on smoking behaviour and birthweight. In: Poswillo, Alberman and Haddow (eds). *Effect of smoking on the fetus neonate and child.* 1991. Oxford University Press.
72. Donovan JW. Randomised controlled trial of antismoking advice in pregnancy. *Br J Prev Soc Med* 1977; **31**: 6–12.
73. MacArthur C, Newton JR, Knox EG. Effect of anti-smoking health education on infant size at birth: a randomised controlled trial. *Br J Obstet Gynaecol* 1987; **94**: 295–300.
74. Oster G, Delea TE, Colditz GA. Maternal smoking during pregnancy and expenditures on neonatal health care. *Am J Prev Med* 1988; 4: 216–9.

Chapter 2: **Passive smoking and the health of children**

1. Fielding JE, Phenow KJ. Health effects of involuntary smoking. *N Engl J Med* 1988; **319**: 1452–60.
2. *Fourth Report of the Independent Scientific Committee on Smoking and Health* (Chairman Sir Peter Froggatt). London: HMSO 1988.
3. Weiss ST, Tager IB, Schenker M, Speizer FE. The health effects of involuntary smoking. *Am Rev Respir Dis* 1983; **128**: 933–42.
4. Jarvis MJ, Russell MAH, Feyerabend C *et al.* Passive exposure to tobacco smoke: saliva cotinine concentrations in a representative population sample of non-smoking schoolchildren. *Br Med J* 1985; **291**: 927–9.
5. Jarvis MJ, McNeill AD, Russell MAH, West RJ, Bryant A, Feyerabend C. Passive smoking in adolescents: one-year stability of exposure in the home. *Lancet* 1987; **i**: 1324–5.
6. Henderson FW, Reid HF, Morris R *et al.* Home air nicotine levels and urinary cotinine excretion in preschool children. *Am Rev Respir Dis* 1989; **140**: 197–201.
7. Strachan DP, Jarvis MJ, Feyerabend C. The relationship of salivary cotinine to respiratory symptoms, spirometry and exercise-induced broncho-spasm in seven-year-old children. *Am Rev Respir Dis* 1990; **142**: 147–51.
8. Coultas DB, Samet JM, McCarthy JF, Spengler JD. Variability of measures of exposure to environmental tobacco smoke in the home. *Am Rev Respir Dis* 1990; **142**: 602–6.
9. Rubin DH, Damus K. The relationship between passive smoking and child health: methodologic criteria applied to prior studies. *Yale J Biol Med* 1988; **61**: 401–11.
10. Taylor B, Wadsworth J. Maternal smoking during pregnancy and lower respiratory tract illness in early life. *Arch Dis Child* 1987; **62**: 786–91.
11. Malloy MH, Kleinman JC, Land GH, Schramm WF. The association of maternal smoking with age and cause of infant death. *Am J Epidemiol* 1988; **128**: 46–55.
12. Haglund B, Cnattingius S. Cigarette smoking as a risk factor for sudden infant death syndrome: a population based study. *Am J Public Health* 1990; **80**: 29–32.
13. Knowelden J, Keeling J, Nicholl JP. *A multicentre study of post-neonatal mortality.* London: HMSO 1985.
14. Office of Population Censuses and Surveys. *Sudden infant death syndrome 1988–89.* OPCS Monitor, DH3 91/1. London: HMSO 1991.

15. Harlap S, Davies AM. Infant admissions to hospital and maternal smoking. *Lancet* 1974; **i**: 529–32.
16. Colley JRT, Holland WW, Corkhill RT. Influence of passive smoking and parental phlegm on pneumonia and bronchitis in early childhood. *Lancet* 1974; **ii**: 1031–4.
17. Fergusson DM, Horwood LJ, Shannon FT. Parental smoking and respiratory illness in infancy. *Arch Dis Child* 1980; **55**: 358–61.
18. Pullan CR, Hey EN. Wheezing, asthma and pulmonary dysfunction 10 years after infection with respiratory syncytial virus in infancy. *Br Med J* 1982; **284**: 1665–9.
19. Wright AL, Holberg C, Martinez FD, Taussig LM, and Group Health Medical Associates. Relationship of parental smoking to wheezing and non-wheezing lower respiratory tract illness in infancy. *J Pediatr* 1991; **118**: 207–14.
20. Chen Y, Li W, Yu S. Influence of passive smoking on admissions for respiratory illness in early childhood. *Br Med J* 1986; **293**: 303–6.
21. Fergusson DM, Horwood LJ. Parental smoking and respiratory illness during early childhood. *Pediatr Pulmonol* 1985; **1**: 99–106.
22. Charlton A. Children's coughs related to parental smoking. *Br Med J* 1984; **288**: 1647–9.
23. Somerville SM, Rona RJ, Chinn S. Passive smoking and respiratory conditions in primary school children. *J Epidemiol Community Health* 1988; **42**: 105–10.
24. Ware JH, Dockery DW, Spiro A, Speizer FE, Ferris BG. Passive smoking, gas cooking and respiratory health of children living in six cities. *Am Rev Respir Dis* 1984; **129**: 366–74.
25. Weitzman M, Gortmacker SL, Walker DK, Sobol A. Maternal smoking and childhood asthma. *Pediatrics* 1990; **85**: 505–11.
26. Neuspiel DR, Rush D, Butler NR, Golding G, Bijur PE, Kurzon M. Parental smoking and post-infancy wheezing in children: a prospective cohort study. *Am J Public Health* 1989; **79**: 168–71.
27. Gortmacker SL, Walker DK, Jacobs FH, Ruch-Ross H. Parental smoking and the risk of childhood asthma. *Am J Public Health* 1982; **72**: 574–9.
28. Evans D, Levison MJ, Feldman CH *et al.* The impact of passive smoking on emergency room visits of urban children with asthma. *Am J Respir Dis* 1987; **135**: 567–72.
29. Murray AB, Morrison BJ. The effect of cigarette smoke from the mother on bronchial hyperresponsiveness and severity of symptoms in children with asthma. *J Allergy Clin Immunol* 1986; **77**: 575–81.
30. Murray AB, Morrison BJ. Passive smoking and the seasonal difference of severity of asthma in children. *Chest* 1988; **94**: 701–8.
31. Murray AB, Morrison BJ. Passive smoking by asthmatics: its greater effect on boys than on girls and on older than younger children. *Pediatrics* 1989; **84**: 451–9.
32. Murray AB, Morrison BJ. It is children with atopic dermatitis who develop asthma more frequently if the mother smokes. *J Allergy Clin Immunol* 1990; **86**: 732–9.
33. Cogswell JJ, Mitchell EB, Alexander J. Parental smoking, breast feeding and respiratory infection in development of allergic diseases. *Arch Dis Child* 1987; **62**: 338–44.
34. Rubin HK. Exposure of children with cystic fibrosis to environmental

tobacco smoke. *N Engl J Med* 1990; **323**: 782–8.
35. Groothuis JR, Gutierrez KM, Lauer BA. RSV infection in children with bronchopulmonary dysplasia. *Pediatrics* 1988; **82**: 199–203.
36. Tager IB. 'Passive smoking' and respiratory health in children—sophistry or cause for concern? *Am Rev Respir Dis* 1986; **133**: 959–61.
37. Tager IB, Weiss ST, Munoz A, Rosner B, Speizer FE. Longitudinal study of maternal smoking and pulmonary function in children. *N Engl J Med* 1983; **309**: 699–703.
38. O'Connor GT, Weiss ST, Tager IB, Speizer FE. The effect of passive smoking on pulmonary function and non-specific bronchial hyperresponsiveness in a population-based sample of children and young adults. *Am Rev Respir Dis* 1987; **135**: 800–4.
39. Martinez FD, Antognoni G, Macri F *et al.* Parental smoking enhances bronchial responsiveness in nine-year-old children. *Am Rev Respir Dis* 1988; **138**: 518–23.
40. Tager IB. Passive smoking, bronchial responsiveness and atopy. *Am Rev Respir Dis* 1988; **138**: 507–9.
41. Kraemer MJ, Marshall SG, Richardson MA. Etiologic factors in the development of chronic middle ear effusions. *Clin Rev Allergy* 1984; **2**: 319–28.
42. Strachan DP, Jarvis MJ, Feyerabend C. Passive smoking, salivary cotinine concentrations, and middle ear effusion in 7-year-old children. *Br Med J* 1989; **298**: 1549–52.
43. Kraemer MJ, Richardson MA, Weiss NS *et al.* Risk factors for persistent middle-ear effusions. Otitis media, catarrh, cigarette smoke exposure and atopy. *J Am Med Assoc* 1983; **249**: 1022–5.
44. Black N. The aetiology of glue-ear—a case-control study. *Int J Pediatr Otorhinolaryngol* 1985; **9**: 121–33.
45. Iversen M, Birch L, Lundqvist GR, Elbrond O. Middle ear effusion in children and the indoor environment. *Arch Environ Health* 1985; **40**: 74–9.
46. Stahlberg MR, Ruuskanen O, Virolainen E. Risk factors for recurrent otitis media. *Pediatr Infect Dis J* 1986; **5**: 30–2.
47. Willatt DJ. Children's sore throats related to parental smoking. *Clin Otolaryngol* 1986; **11**: 317–21.
48. Corbo GM, Fuciarelli F, Foresi A, De Benedetto F. Snoring in children: association with respiratory symptoms and passive smoking. *Br Med J* 1989; **299**: 1491–4.
49. Said G, Zalokar J, Lellouch J, Patois E. Parental smoking related to adenoidectomy and tonsillectomy in children. *J Epidemiol Community Health* 1978; **32**: 97–101.
50. Berkey SC, Ware JH, Speizer FE, Ferris BG. Passive smoking and height growth of preadolescent children. *Int J Epidemiol* 1984; **13**: 454–8.
51. Rona RJ, Chinn S, Florey CD. Exposure to cigarette smoking and children's growth. *Int J Epidemiol* 1985; **14**: 402–9.
52. Rantakillio P. Relationship of maternal smoking to morbidity and mortality of the child up to the age of five. *Acta Paediatr Scand* 1978; **67**: 621–31.
53. Golding J, Butler NR. Chaper 17: Hospital admissions. In: *Birth to five*. Oxford: Pergamon Press 1986.
54. Charlton A, Blair V. Absence from school related to children's and parental smoking habits. *Br Med J* 1989; **298**: 90–2.
55. Moskowitz WB, Mosteller M, Schieken RM *et al.* Lipoprotein and oxygen

transport alterations in passive smoking preadolescent children. *Circulation* 1990; **81**: 586–92.

56. Sandler DP, Wilcox AJ, Everson RB. Cumulative effects of lifetime passive smoking on cancer risk. *Lancet* 1985; **i**: 312–5.
57. Wald NW, Booth C, Doll R *et al* (eds). *Passive smoking—a health hazard.* London: Imperial Cancer Research Fund and Cancer Research Campaign 1991.
58. General Household Survey 1988. London: OPCS 1990.

Chapter 3: **Active smoking and the health effects for children**

1. US Department of Health and Human Services. *The health consequences of smoking: nicotine addiction.* A report of the Surgeon General (DHHS publication No. (PHS) 88-8406). 1988. Atlanta Centres for Disease Control, Centre for Health Promotion and Education, Office on Smoking and Health.
2. Benowitz NL. Pharmacokinetic considerations in understanding nicotine dependence. In: *The biology of nicotine dependence.* Ciba Foundation Symposium 152. Chichester: Wiley 1990; 186–209.
3. Benowitz NL, Jacob P III. Daily intake of nicotine during cigarette smoking. *Clin Pharmacol Ther* 1984; **35**: 499–504.
4. Kato S, Wakasa Y, Yanagita T. Relationship between minimum reinforcing doses and injection speed in cocaine and pentobarbital self-administration in crab-eating monkeys. *Pharmacol Biochem Behav* 1987; **28**: 407–10.
5. Gritz ER. Patterns of puffing in cigarette smokers. In: Drasnegor NA (ed). *Self-administration of abused substances: methods for study* (NIDA Research Monograph 20). Rockville, Maryland: National Institute on Drug Abuse 1978; 221–35.
6. US Department of Health and Human Services. *Drug abuse and drug abuse research.* Second triennial report to Congress from the Secretary, Department of Health and Human Services (DHHS publication No. (ADM) 87-1468). Washington DC: US Government Printing Office, 1987.
7. McNeill AD. The development of dependence on smoking in children. *Br J Addict* 1991; **86**: 589–92.
8. McNeill AD, Jarvis MJ, Stapleton JA, West RJ, Bryant A. Nicotine intake in young mothers: longitudinal study of saliva cotinine concentrations. *Am J Public Health* 1989; **79**: 172–5.
9. McNeill AD, West RJ, Jarvis MJ, Jackson P, Russell MAH. Cigarette withdrawal symptoms in adolescent smokers. *Psychopharmacology* 1986; **90**: 533–6.
10. McNeill AD, Jarvis MJ, West RJ. Subjective effects of cigarette smoking in adolescents. *Psychopharmacology* 1987; **92**: 115–7.
11. MORI/HEA *Teenage health and lifestyles study: smoking.* Unpublished.
12. Burton D. *Who identifies a smoker?* Background paper prepared for International Workshop of Children and Tobacco in Industrialised Countries, Toronto. Available from UICC, Geneva.
13. Andrae S, Axelson O, Bjorksten B. Symptoms of bronchial hyperreactivity

and asthma in relation to environmental factors. *Arch Dis Child* 1983; **63**: 473–8.

14. Tager IB, Minnoz A, Rosner B, Weiss ST, Carey V, Speizer FE. Effect of cigarette smoking on the pulmonary function of children and adolescents. *Am Rev Respir Dis* 1985; **131**: 752–9.

15. Woolcock AJ, Peat JK, Leeder SR, Blackburn CRB. The development of lung function in Sydney children: effects of respiratory illness and smoking. A ten year study. *Eur J Respir Dis* 1984; **65**: suppl 132.

16. Oechsli FW, Seltzer CC, van den Berg BJ. Adolescent smoking and early respiratory disease: a longitudinal study. *Ann Allergy* 1987; **59**: 135–40.

17. Martin AJ, Landau LI, Phelan PD. Asthma from childhood to age 21: the patient and his disease. *Br Med J* 1982; **284**: 380–2.

18. Stanhope JM, Prior IAM. Smoking behaviour and respiratory health in a teenage sample: the Rotorua Lakes Study. *NZ Med J* 1975; **82**: 71–6.

19. Rawbone RG, Keeling CA, Jenkins H, Guz A. Cigarette smoking among secondary schoolchildren in 1975. *J Epidemiol Community Health* 1978; **32**: 53–8.

20. Parnell JL, Anderson DO, Kinnis C. Cigarette smoking and respiratory infections in a class of student nurses. *N Engl J Med* 1966; **274**: 979–84.

21. Charlton A, Blair V. Absence from school related to children's and parental smoking habits. *Br Med J* 1989; **298**: 90–2.

22. Haynes WF, Krstulovic VJ, Bell ALL. Smoking habit and incidence of respiratory tract infections in a group of adolescent males. *Am Rev Respir Dis* 1966; **93**: 730–4.

23. Kujala P. Smoking, respiratory symptoms and ventilatory capacity in young men. *Eur J Respir Dis* 1981; **62**: suppl 114.

24. Bewley BR, Halil T, Snaith AH. Smoking by primary school children: prevalence and associated respiratory symptoms. *Br J Prev Soc Med* 1973; **27**: 150–3.

25. Bewley BR, Bland JM. Smoking and respiratory symptoms in two groups of schoolchildren. *Prev Med* 1976; **5**: 63–9.

26. Colley JRT, Douglas JWB, Reid DD. Respiratory disease in young adults: influence of early childhood lower respiratory tract illness, social class, air pollution, and smoking. *Br Med J* 1973; **3**: 195–8.

27. Rush D. Respiratory symptoms in a group of American secondary school students: the overwhelming association with cigarette smoking. *Int J Epidemiol* 1974; **3**: 723–65.

28. Rimpela AH, Rimpela MK. Increased risk of respiratory symptoms in young smokers of low tar cigarettes. *Br Med J* 1985; **290**: 1461–3.

29. Rush D. Changes in respiratory symptoms related to smoking in a teenage population: the results of two linked surveys separated by one year. *Int J Epidemiol* 1976; **5**: 173–8.

30. Adams L, Lonsdale D, Robinson M, Rawbone R, Guz A. Respiratory impairment induced by smoking in children in secondary schools. *Br Med J* 1984; **288**: 891–5.

31. Rees PJ, Ayres JG, Chowienczyk PJ, Clark TJH. Irritant effects of cigarette and cigar smoke. *Lancet* 1982; **ii**: 1015–7.

32. Peters JM, Ferris BG. Smoking, pulmonary function and respiratory symptoms in a college age-group. *Am Rev Respir Dis* 1967; **95**: 774–82.

33. Walter S, Nancy NR, Collier CR. Changes in the forced expiratory spirogram in young male smokers. *Am Rev Respir Dis* 1979; **119**: 117–24.

34. Tashkin DP, Clark VA, Coulson AH, Bourque LB, Simmons M, Reems C, Detels R, Rokaw S. Comparison of lung function in young non-smokers and smokers before and after initiation of the smoking habit. A prospective study. *Am Rev Respir Dis* 1983; **128**: 12–6.

35. Jaakola MS, Ernst P, Jaakola JJK, N'gan'ga LW, Becklake MR. Effect of cigarette smoking on evolution of ventilatory function in young adults: an eight year longitudinal study. *Thorax* 1991; **46**: 907–13.

36. Lim TPK. Airway obstruction amongst high school students. *Am Rev Respir Dis* 1973; **108**: 985–8.

37. Corbin RP, Loveland M, Martin RR, Macklem PT. A four-year follow-up study of lung mechanics in smokers. *Am Rev Respir Dis* 1979; **120**: 293–304.

38. Buist S, Vollmer WM, Johnson LR, McCamont LR. Does the single breath N_2 test identify the smoker who will develop chronic airflow limitation? *Am Rev Respir Dis* 1988; **137**: 293–301.

39. Lebowitz MD, Holberg CJ, Knudsom RJ, Burrows B. Longitudinal study of pulmonary function development in childhood, adolescence, and early adulthood. Development of pulmonary function. *Am Rev Respir Dis* 1987; **136**: 69–75.

40. Jaakola MS, Jaakola JJK, Ernst P, Becklake MR. Ventilatory lung function in young cigarette smokers: a study of susceptibility. *Eur Respir J* 1991; **4**: 643–50.

41. Tockman M, Menkes H, Cohen B, Permutt S, Benjamin J, Ball WL, Tonascia J. A comparison of pulmonary function in male smokers and non-smokers. *Am Rev Respir Dis* 1976; **114**: 711–22.

42. Buist AS, van Fleet DL, Ross BB. A comparison of conventional spirometric tests and the test of closing volume in an emphysema screening centre. *Am Rev Respir Dis* 1973; **107**: 735–43.

43. Beck GJ, Doyle CA, Schachter EN. Smoking and lung function. *Am Rev Respir Dis* 1981; **123**: 149–55.

44. Tager IB, Segal MR, Speizer FE, Weiss ST. The natural history of forced expiratory volumes: effect of cigarette smoke and respiratory symptoms. *Am Rev Respir Dis* 1988; **138**: 837–49.

45. Reynolds HY, Merrill WW. Airway changes in young smokers that antedate chronic obstructive lung disease. *Med Clin North Am* 1981; **65**: 667–90.

46. Goodman RM, Yergin BM, Landa JF, Golinvaux MH, Sackner MA. Relationship of smoking history and pulmonary function tests to tracheal muscle velocity in non-smokers, young smokers, ex-smokers and patients with chronic bronchitis. *Am Rev Respir Dis* 1978; **117**: 305–14.

47. Niewoehner DE, Kleinerman J, Rice DB. Pathologic changes in the peripheral airways of young cigarette smokers. *N Engl J Med* 1974; **291**: 755–8.

48. Peto R. Influence of dose and duration of smoking on lung cancer rates. In: Zarridge DG, Peto R (eds). *Tobacco: a major international health hazard*. Lyon, France: International Agency for Research on Cancer 1986; 23–33.

49. Trap-Jensen J. Effects of smoking on the heart and peripheral circulation. *Am Heart J* 1988; **115**: 263–6.

50. West RJ, Russell MAH. Cardiovascular and subjective effects of smoking before and after 24 hr abstinence from cigarettes. *Psychopharmacology*

1987; **92**: 118–21.
51. Bounameaux H, Griessen M, Benedet P, Krahenbuhl AD. Nicotine induced haemodynamic changes during cigarette smoking and nicotine gum chewing: a placebo controlled study in young healthy volunteers. *Cardiovasc Res* 1988; **22**: 154–8.
52. Bekheit S, Fletcher E. The effects of smoking on myocardial conduction in the human heart. *Am Heart J* 1976; **91**: 712–20.
53. McHenry PL, Faris JV, Jordan JW, Morris SN. Comparative study of cardiovascular function and ventricular premature complexes in smokers and non-smokers during maximal treadmill exercise. *Am J Cardiol* 1977; **39**: 493–8.
54. Lewis RP, Boudoulas H. Catecholamines, cigarette smoking, arrhythmias, and acute myocardial infarction. *Am Heart J* 1974; **88**: 526–7.
55. Davis MJE, Hockings EF, El Dessouky MAM, Hajar HA, Taylor RR. Cigarette smoking and ventricular arrhythmia in coronary heart disease. *Am J Cardiol* 1984; **54**: 282–5.
56. Dembroski TM, MacDougall JM, Cardozo SR, Ireland SK, Krug-Fite J. Selective cardiovascular effects of stress and cigarette smoking in young women. *Health Psychol* 1985; **4**: 153–67.
57. Stone SV, Dembroski TM, Costa PT, MacDougall JM. Gender differences in cardiovascular reactivity. *J Behav Med* 1990; **13**: 137–56.
58. Emmons KM, Weidner G. The effects of cognitive and physical stress on cardiovascular reactivity among smokers and oral contraceptive users. *Psychophysiology* 1988; **25**: 166–71.
59. Laustiola KE, Lassila R, Kaprio J, Kostenvuo M. Decreased β-adrenergic receptor density and catecholamine response in male cigarette smokers. A study of monozygotic twin pairs discordant for smoking. *Circulation* 1988; **78**: 1234–40.
60. Blake GH, Parker JA. Success in basic combat training: the role of cigarette smoking. *J Occup Med* 1991; **33**: 688–90.
61. Cooper KH, Gey GO, Bottenberg RA. Effects of cigarette smoking on endurance performance. *J Am Med Assoc* 1968; **203**: 123–6.
62. Marti B, Abelin T, Minder CE, Vader JP. Smoking, alcohol consumption and endurance capacity: an analysis of 6,500 19-year-old conscripts and 4,100 joggers. *Prev Med* 1988; **17**: 79–92.
63. Klausen K, Andersen C, Nandrup S. Acute effects of cigarette smoking and inhalation of carbon monoxide during maximal exercise. *Eur J Appl Physiol* 1983; **51**: 371–9.
64. Gordon DJ, Leon AS, Ekelund L-G, Sopko G, Probstfield JL, Rubenstein C, Sheffield LT. Smoking, physical activity and other predictors of endurance and heart rate response to exercise in asymptomatic hypercholesterolemic men. *Am J Epidemiol* 1987; **125**: 587–600.
65. Hirsch GL, Sue DY, Wasserman K, Robinson TE, Hansen JE. Immediate effects of cigarette smoking on cardiorespiratory responses to exercise. *J Appl Physiol* 1985; **58**: 1975–81.
66. Davis JW, Shelton L, Eigenberg DA, Hignite CE, Watanabe IS. Effects of tobacco and non-tobacco cigarette smoking on endothelium and platelets. *Clin Pharmacol Ther* 1985; **37**: 529–33.
67. Schmidt KG, Rasmussen JW. Acute platelet activation induced by smoking: *in vivo* and *ex vivo* studies in humans. *Thromb Haemost* 1984; **51**: 279–82.

68. Pittilo RM, Clarke JMF, Harris D, Mackie IJ, Rowles PM, Machin SJ, Woolf N. Cigarette smoking and platelet adhesion. *Br J Haematol* 1984; **58**: 627–32.
69. Rangemark C, Wennmalm A. Cigarette smoking and urinary excretion of markers for platelet/vessel wall interaction in healthy women. *Clin Sci* 1991; **81**: 11–5.
70. Lassila R, Seyberth HW, Haapanen A, Schweer H, Koskenvuo M, Laustiola KE. Vasoactive and atherogenic effects of cigarette smoking: a study of monozygotic twins discordant for smoking. *Br Med J* 1988; **297**: 955–7.
71. Nowak J, Murray JJ, Oates JA, Fitzgerald GA. Biochemical evidence of a chronic abnormality in platelet and vascular function in healthy individuals who smoke cigarettes. *Circulation* 1987; **76**: 6–14.
72. Nadler JL, Velasco JS, Horton R. Cigarette smoking inhibits prostacyclin formation. *Lancet* 1983; **i**: 1248–50.
73. Stoel I, Giessen WJ, Wolsman EZ, Verheught FWA, Hoor F, Quadt FJA, Hugenholtz PG. Effect of nicotine on production of prostacyclin in human umbilical artery. *Br Heart J* 1982; **48**: 493–6.
74. Allen RA, Kluft C, Brommer EJP. Acute effect of smoking on fibrinolysis: increase in the activity level of circulating extrinsic (tissue-type) plasminogen activator. *Eur J Clin Invest* 1984; **14**: 354–61.
75. Hashimoto Y, Kobayashi A, Yamazaki N, Takada Y, Takada A. Relationship between smoking and fibrinolytic system with special reference to t-PA and PA inhibitor. *Thromb Res* 1988; **51**: 303–11.
76. Belch JJF, McArdle BM, Burns P, Lowe GDO, Forbes CD. The effects of acute smoking on platelet behaviour, fibrinolysis and haemorheology in habitual smokers. *Thromb Haemost* 1984; **51**: 6–8.
77. Markowe HLJ, Marmot MG, Shipley MJ, Bulpitt CJ, Meade TW, Stirling Y, Vickers MV, Semmence A. Fibrinogen: a possible link between social class and coronary heart disease. *Br Med J* 1985; **291**: 1312–4.
78. Kannel WB, D'Agostino RB, Belander AJ. Fibrinogen, cigarette smoking and risk of cardiovascular disease: insights from the Framingham study. *Am Heart J* 1987; **113**: 1006–10.
79. Dotevall A, Kutti J, Teger-Nilsson A-C, Wadenvik H, Wilhelmsen L. Platelet reactivity, fibrinogen and smoking. *Eur J Haematol* 1987; **38**: 55–9.
80. Yarnell JWG, Fehily AM, Milbank J, Kubicki AJ, Eastham R, Hyes TM. Determinants of plasma lipoproteins and coagulation factors in men from Caerphilly, South Wales. *J Epidemiol Community Health* 1983; **37**: 137–40.
81. Feher MD, Rampling MW, Brown J, Robinson R, Richmond W, Cholerton S, Bain BJ, Sever PS. Acute changes in atherogenic and thrombogenic factors with cessation of smoking. *J R Soc Med* 1990; **83**: 146–8.
82. Galea G, Davidson RJL. Haematological and haemorheological changes associated with cigarette smoking. *J Clin Pathol* 1985; **38**: 978–84.
83. Meade TW, Imeson J, Stirling Y. Effects of changes in smoking and other characteristics on clotting factors and the risk of ischaemic heart disease. *Lancet* 1987; **ii**: 986–8.
84. Elkeles RS, Khan SR, Chowdhury V, Swallow MB. Effects of smoking on oral fat tolerance and high density lipoprotein cholesterol. *Clin Sci* 1983; **65**: 669–72.
85. Craig WY, Palomaki GE, Haddow JE. Cigarette smoking and serum lipid

and lipoprotein concentrations: an analysis of published data. *Br Med J* 1989; **298**: 784–8.

86. Neaton JD, Kuller LH, Wentworth D, Borhani NO. Total and cardio-vascular mortality in relation to cigarette smoking, serum cholesterol concentration, and diastolic blood pressure among black and white males followed up for five years. *Am Heart J* 1984; **108**: 759–69.

87. Davies MJ. The pathology of acute myocardial infarction and sudden ischaemic death. In: Sobel BE, Julian DG, Hugenholtz PG (eds). *Perspectives in cardiology.* London: Current Medical Literature 1988.

88. ISIS-2 Collaborative Group. Randomised trial of intravenous streptokinase, oral aspirin, both or neither among 17,187 cases of suspected acute myocardial infarction. ISIS 2. *Lancet* 1988; **ii**: 349–60.

89. Antiplatelet Trialists Collaboration. Secondary prevention of vascular disease by prolonged antiplatelet treatment. *Br Med J* 1988; **296**: 320–31.

90. Tomono S, Ohshima S, Murata K. The risk factors for ischaemic heart disease in young adults. *Jpn Circ J* 1990; **54**: 436–41.

91. Kaul U, Dogra B, Manchanda SC, Wasir HS, Rajani M, Bhatia ML. Myocardial infarction in young Indian patients: risk factors and coronary arteriographic profile. *Am Heart J* 1986; **112**: 71–5.

92. Kennelly BM. Aetiology and risk factors in young patients with recent acute myocardial infarction. *S Afr Med J* 1982; **61**: 503–7.

93. Hayat N, Mohamed M, Simo M. Coronary artery disease in patients aged 30 and younger. *Jpn Heart J* 1986; **27**: 679–84.

94. Weinberger I, Rotenberg Z, Fuchs J, Sagy A, Friedman J, Agmon J. Myocardial infarction in young adults under 30 years: risk factors and clinical course. *Clin Cardiol* 1987; **10**: 9–15.

95. Daly LE, Mulcahy R, Graham IM, Hickey N. Long term effect on mortality of stopping smoking after unstable angina and myocardial infarction. *Br Med J* 1983; **287**: 324–6.

96. Perkins J, Dick TBC. Smoking and myocardial infarction: secondary prevention. *Postgrad Med J* 1985; **61**: 295–300.

97. Vliestra RE, Kronmal RA, Oberman A, Frye RL, Killip T. Effect of cigarette smoking on survival of patients with angiographically documented coronary artery disease. *J Am Med Assoc* 1986; **255**: 1023–7.

98. Henrich JB, Horwitz RI. The contributions of individual factors to thromboembolic stroke. *J Gen Intern Med* 1989; **4**: 195–201.

99. Love BB, Biller J, Jones MP, Adams HP, Bruno A. Cigarette smoking: a risk factor for cerebral infarction in young adults. *Arch Neurol* 1990; **47**: 693–8.

100. Wolf PA, D'Agostino RB, Kannel WB, Bonita R, Belanger AJ. Cigarette smoking as a risk factor for stroke. *J Am Med Assoc* 1988; **259**: 1025–9.

101. Taha A, Ball KP, Illingworth RD. Smoking and subarachnoid haemorrhage. *J R Soc Med* 1982; **75**: 332–5.

102. Pettiti DH, Wingerd J. Use of oral contraceptives, cigarette smoking and risk of subarachnoid haemorrhage. *Lancet* 1978; **ii**: 234–6.

103. Bell BA, Symon L. Smoking and subarachnoid haemorrhage. *Br Med J* 1979; **i**: 577–8.

104. Oleckno WA. The risk of stroke in young adults: an analysis of the contribution of cigarette smoking and alcohol consumption. *Public Health* 1988; **102**: 45–55.

105. Hughson WG, Mann JI, Tibbs DJ, Woods HF, Walton I. Intermittent

claudication: factors determining outcome. *Br Med J* 1978; **i**: 1377–9.
106. Wiseman S, Kenchington G, Dain R, Marshall CE, McCollum CN, Greenhalgh RM, Powell JT. Influence of smoking and plasma factors on patency of femoropopliteal vein grafts. *Br Med J* 1989; **299**: 643–6.
107. Solymoss BC, Nadeau P, Millette D, Campeau L. Late thrombosis of saphenous vein coronary bypass grafts related to risk factors. *Circulation* 1988; **78** (supplement I): I-140–3.
108. Lassila R, Lepantalo M. Cigarette smoking and the outcome after lower limb arterial surgery. *Acta Chir Scand* 1988; **154**: 535–40.
109. Buerger L. Thrombo-angiitis obliterans: a study of the vascular lesions leading to presenile spontaneous gangrene. *Am J Med Sci* 1908; **136**: 567–80.
110. Hopkins PN, Williams RR. Identification and relative weight of cardiovascular risk factors. *Cardiol Clin* 1986; **4**: 3–31.
111. United States Surgeon General. *The health consequences of smoking: cardiovascular disease*. Rockville, Maryland: United States Department of Health and Human Services 1983.
112. Von Wyk CW. An oral pathology profile of a group of juvenile delinquents. *J Forensic Odontostomatol* 1983; **1**(1): 3–10.
113. Kandunce D. Cigarette smoking: risk factors for premature facial wrinkling. *Ann Int Med* 1991; **14**: 840–4.
114. Sherman CB. Health effects of cigarette smoking. *Clin Chest Med* 1991; **12**: 643–58.
115. Holt PG. Immune and inflammatory function in cigarette smokers. *Thorax* 1987; **42**: 241–9.
116. Halsey NA, Coberly JS, Holt EH *et al*. Sexual behaviour, smoking and HIV-1 infection in Haitian women. *J Am Med Assoc* 1992; **267**: 2062–6.
117. Nieman R, Fleming J, Coker RJ, Hains JRW, Mitchell DM. *Cigarette smoking by HIV infected individuals is associated with more rapid progression to AIDS*. VIII Int Conference on AIDS. Amsterdam, July 1992.

Chapter 4: **Prevalence and development of smoking in young people**

1. Lader D, Matheson J. *Smoking among secondary school children in 1990*. OPCS. London: HMSO 1991.
2. Charlton A, Gillies P, Ledwith F. Variations between schools and regions in smoking prevalence among British schoolchildren. *Public Health* 1985; **99**: 243–9.
3. Murray M, Kiryluk S, Swan AV. School characteristics and adolescent smoking. Results from the MRC Derbyshire smoking study 1974–1977 and from a follow-up in 1981. *J Epidemiol Community Health* 1984; **38**: 167–72.
4. Bewley BR, Day I, Ide L. *Smoking by children in Great Britain*. London: Social Science Research Council and Medical Research Council 1973.
5. General Household Survey. *Cigarette smoking 1972–1990*. General Household Survey Monitor SS91/3. London: OPCS 1991.
6. ASH Women and Smoking Group. *Teenage girls and smoking*. London: Action on Smoking and Health 1989.
7. Charlton A. Clues to planning smoking education for the 16 plus age group on vocational courses. *Health Educ J* 1983; **42**: 71–3.

8. McNeill AD, Jarvis MJ, Stapleton JA, Russell MAH, Eiser JR, Gammage P, Gray EM. Prospective study of factors predicting uptake of smoking in adolescents. *J Epidemiol Community Health* 1988; **43**: 72–8.
9. McNeill AD, West RJ, Jarvis M, Jackson P, Bryant A. Cigarette withdrawal symptoms in adolescent smokers. *Psychopharmacology* 1986; **90**: 533–6.
10. Doll R, Peto R. *The causes of cancer.* Oxford: Oxford University Press 1981.
11. US Department of Health and Human Services. *The health consequences of smoking: cardiovascular disease.* A report of the Surgeon General. Rockville, Maryland: US Department of Health and Human Services, Public Health Service, Office on Smoking and Health 1983.
12. Flay BR, D'Avernas JR, Best JA, Kersell MW, Ryan KB. Cigarette smoking: why do young people do it and ways of preventing it. In: McGrath PJ, Firestone P (eds). *Pediatric and adolescent behavioral medicine.* New York: Springer-Verlag 1983; 132–83.
13. Stern RA, Prochaska JO, Velicer WF, Elder JP. Stages of adolescent cigarette smoking acquisition. *Addict Behav* 1987; **12**: 319–29.
14. Murray M, Swan AV, Johnson MRD, Bewley BR. Some factors associated with increased risk of smoking by children. *J Child Psychol Psychiatry* 1983; **24**: 223–32.
15. Baugh JG, Hunter S MacD, Webber LS, Berenson GS. Developmental trends of first cigarette smoking experience of children: the Bogalusa heart study. *Am J Public Health* 1982; **72**: 1161–4.
16. Becker MH. The health belief model and personal health behaviour. *Health Educ Monographs* 1974; **2**: 324–508.
17. Fishbein M, Ajzen J. *Belief, attitude, intention and behaviour.* New York: Addison-Wesley 1985.
18. Bandura A. Analysis of self-efficacy theory of behavioural change. *Cogn Ther Res* 1977; **1**: 287–308.
19. Maier H. *Three theories of child development.* New York: Harper and Row 1969.
20. Aitken PP. Peer group pressure, parental control and cigarette smoking among 10 to 14 year olds. *Br J Soc Clin Psychol* 1980; **19**: 141–6.
21. Jessor R. Problem behaviour and developmental transition in adolescence. *J Sch Health* 1982; **23**: 189–99.
22. De Vries H, Djikstra M, Kuhlman P. Self-efficacy: the third factor beside attitude and subjective norm as a predictor of behavioural intentions. *Health Educ Res* 1988; **3**: 273–82.
23. Lloyd P. *Self-esteem and smoking in 11 to 13 year olds.* Manchester: MSc thesis, University of Manchester 1989.
24. Piaget J. *The psychology of the child.* New York: Basic Books 1969.
25. Lowrey GH. *Growth and development in children.* Chicago: Year Book Medical Publishers 1978.
26. Charlton A. Children's opinions on smoking. *J R Coll Gen Pract* 1984; **34**: 483–7.

Chapter 5: **Personal and social factors influencing smoking**

1. Charlton A, Melia P, Moyer (C (eds). *A manual on tobacco and young people for the industrialised world.* Geneva: International Union Against Cancer 1990.

2. Jessor R. Problem behaviour and developmental transition in adolescence. *J Sch Health* 1982; **52**: 295–300.
3. Flay BR, d'Avernas JR, Best JA, Kersell MW, Ryan KB. Cigarette smoking: why young people do it and ways of preventing it. In: McGrath P, Firestone P (eds). *Pediatric and adolescent behavioral medicine*. New York: Springer-Verlag 1983; 132–83.
4. Chassin L, Presson CC, Sherman SJ, Corty E, Olshavsky RW. Predicting the onset of cigarette smoking in adolescents: a longitudinal study. *J Appl Soc Psychol* 1984; **14**: 224–43.
5. Plant MA, Peck DF, Samuel E. *Alcohol, drugs and school leavers*. London: Tavistock 1985.
6. Wills TA. Stress and coping in early adolescence relationships to substance use in urban school samples. *Health Psychol* 1986; **5**: 503–29.
7. Castro FG, Maddahion E, Newcomb MD, Bentler PM. A multivariate model of the determinants of cigarette smoking among adolescents. *J Health Soc Behav* 1987; **2**: 273–89.
8. Gillies PA, Galt M. Teenage smoking—fun or coping? In: Winnbust JAM, Maes S (eds). *Lifestyles and health: new developments in health psychology*. DSWO/LEIDEW. Netherlands University Press 1991.
9. Thompson EL. Smoking education programs, 1960–76. *Am J Public Health* 1978; **68**: 250–7.
10. Charlton A, Blair V. Predicting the onset of smoking in boys and girls. *Soc Sci Med* 1989; **29**: 813–8.
11. Bland JM, Bewley BR, Banks MH, Pollard V. Schoolchildren's beliefs about smoking and disease. *Health Educ J* 1975; **34**: 71–8.
12. Charlton A. Lung cancer: the ultimate smoking deterrent for young people? *J Inst Health Educ* 1982; **20**: 5–12.
13. Reid D. Prevention of smoking among school children: recommendations for policy development. *Health Educ J* 1985; **44**: 3–12.
14. Tones BK. Health promotion, effective education and the personal-social development of young people. In: David K, Williams T (eds). *Health education in schools*. London: Harper and Row 1987.
15. Murray M, Swan AV, Johnson MRD, Bewley BR. Some factors associated with increased risk of smoking by children. *J Child Psychol Psychiatry* 1983; **24**: 223–32.
16. Bewley BR, Bland JM, Harris R. Factors associated with the starting of cigarette smoking by primary school children. *Br J Prev Soc Med* 1974; **28**: 37–44.
17. Charlton A. The Brigantia Smoking Survey: a general review. *Public education about cancer*. UICC Technical Report Series 1984; **77**: 92–102.
18. Murray M, Kiryluk S, Swan AV. Relation between parents' and children's smoking behaviour and attitudes. *J Epidemiol Community Health* 1985; **39**: 169–74.
19. Charlton A. Children who smoke. *Health at School* 1986; **1**: 125–7.
20. Eiser JR, Morgan M, Gammage P, Gray E. Adolescent smoking: attitudes, norms and parental influence. *Br J Soc Physiol* 1989; **28**: 193–202.
21. Nelson SC, Budd RJ, Eiser JR, Morgan M, Gammage P, Gray E. The Avon prevalence study: a survey of cigarette smoking in secondary schoolchildren. *Health Educ. J* 1985; **44**: 12–5.
22. McGuffin SJ. Smoking—the knowledge and behaviour of young people in Northern Ireland. *Health Educ J* 1982; **41**: 53–9.

23. Murray M, Swan AV, Bewley BR, Johnson MRD. The development of smoking during adolescence—the MRC/Derbyshire smoking study. *Int J Epidemiol* 1984; **12**: 185–92.
24. Marsh A, Matheson J. *Smoking attitudes and behaviour*. London: HMSO 1983.
25. Graham H. Women's smoking and family health. *Soc Sci Med* 1987; **25**: 47–56.
26. Charlton A. Smoking in one parent families. *Progress in public education about cancer: international perspectives* 1991; **2**: 13–9.
27. Green G, MacIntyre S, West P, Ecob R. Do children of lone parents smoke more because their mothers do? *Br J Addict* 1990; **85**: 1497–500.
28. MORI. *Teenage health and lifestyles study: smoking* (unpublished) 1989. London: Health Education Authority.
29. Kohli HS. A comparison of smoking and drinking among Asian and white schoolchildren in Glasgow. *Public Health* 1989; **103**: 433–9.
30. Murray M, McReynolds F. Cigarette smoking among 11–12 year olds in the western area of Northern Ireland: family and school factors. *Public Health* 1987; **101**: 465–71.
31. Riggs S, Alano AJ, McHoney C. Health risk behaviours and attempted suicides in adolescents who report prior maltreatment. *J Pediatr* 1990; **1.6(5)**: 815–21.
32. McNeill AD, Jarvis MJ, Stapleton JA, Russell MAH, Eiser JR, Gammage P, Gray EH. Prospective study of factors predicting uptake of smoking in adolescents. *J Epidemiol Community Health* 1988; **43**: 72–8.
33. Goddard E. *Why children start smoking*. London: HMSO 1990.
34. Mittlemark MB, Murray DM, Luepker RV, Pechacek JF, Pirie PL, Pallonan HE. Predicting experimentation with cigarettes. The childhood antecedents of smoking study. *Am J Public Health* 1987; **77**: 206–8.
35. McAlister A, Perry C, Maccoby N. Adolescents' smoking—onset and prevention. *Pediatrics* 1979; **63**: 650–8.
36. Banks MH, Bewley BR, Bland JM. Adolescent attitudes to smoking: their influence on behaviour. *Int J Health Educ* 1981; **24**: 39–44.
37. Bewley BR, Johnson MRD, Banks MH. Teachers' smoking. *J Epidemiol Community Health* 1979; **33**: 219–22.
38. Cancer Research Campaign. *Smoking policies and prevalence for 16 to 19 year olds in schools and colleges*. A report by Public Attitude Surveys Ltd. London: Cancer Research Campaign 1991.
39. Porter A. Disciplinary attitudes and cigarette smoking: a comparison of two schools. *Br Med J* 1982: **286**: 1725–6.
40. Murray M, Kiryluk S, Swan AV. School characteristics and adolescent smoking. *J Epidemiol Community Health* 1984; **38**: 167–72.
41. Hilton S. Smoking ban set for city schools. *Birmingham Evening Mail* 22 July 1991.
42. Brueckner E. Memorandum on 4th World Conference on Smoking and Health (20 June 1979). ASH Information Library.
43. Wald NW, Booth C, Doll R *et al* (eds). *Passive smoking—a health hazard*. London: Imperial Cancer Research Fund and Cancer Research Campaign 1991.
44. Royal College of Physicians. *Health or smoking?* London: Royal College of Physicians 1983.
45. NOP. *London Evening Standard* 27 July 1987.

46. MORI. *Survey of personnel directors*. BUPA, July 1990.
47. NOP. *Smoking habits*. Survey for Department of Health, 1990.
48. Batten L. *Managing change: smoking policies in the NHS*. London: Health Education Authority 1990.
49. Batten L, Allen S. *Towards a smoke-free environment: local authority policies and practice*. London: Health Education Authority 1991.
50. *Smoking in public places*. Department of Environment, 91 EP 0176, December 1991.
51. *Health update—smoking*. London: Health Education Authority 1991.
52. Cigarettes. Market Intelligence, December 1990. Mintel, 1990.
53. CTN. 2 August 1990.
54. *Smoking among secondary school children in England in 1988*. OPCS 1989.
55. Parents against tobacco. *Newsletter*. January 1990.
56. *Criminal statistics England and Wales*. CM1322. London: HMSO 1989.
57. Townsend J. Tobacco price and the smoking epidemic. *Smoke-free Europe: 9*. Copenhagen: WHO 1988.
58. Lewit EM, Coate D, Grossman M. The effects of government regulations on teenage smoking. *J Law Econ* 1981; **14**: 545–69.
59. Townsend J. Economic and health consequences of reduced smoking. In: Williams A (ed). *Health and economics*. London: Macmillan 1987.

Chapter 6: **Intervention strategies**

1. Department of Health. *The health of the nation: a consultative document for health in England*. London: HMSO 1991.
2. Scottish Office Home and Health Department. *Health education in Scotland: a national statement*. Edinburgh: HMSO 1991.
3. Health Promotion Authority for Wales. *Health for all in Wales: health promotion challenges for the 1990s*. Cardiff: Health Promotion Authority for Wales 1990.
4. World Health Organisation. Ottawa Charter. *Health promotion—an international journal*. 1986; Vol 1, No 4.
5. Thompson EL. Smoking education programmes, 1960–76. *Am J Public Health* 1978; **68**: 250–7.
6. Nutbeam D. *Planning for a smoke-free generation. Smoke-free Europe: 6*. Copenhagen: World Health Organisation Regional Office for Europe 1988.
7. Gillies PA, Wilcox B. Reducing the risk of smoking amongst the young. *Public Health* 1984; **98**: 49–54.
8. McGuire WJ. Inducing resistance to persuasion. In: Berkowitz L (ed). *Advances in experimental social psychology* Vol 1. New York: Academic Press 1965.
9. Evans RI *et al*. Social modelling films to deter smoking in adolescents: results of a three year field investigation. *J Appl Psychol* 1981; **66**: 399–414.
10. Vartiainen E *et al*. Effect of two years of educational intervention in adolescent smoking (the North Karelia Youth Project). *Bulletin of the World Health Organisation* 1983; **61**(3): 529–32.
11. Tell GS, Klepp KI, Vellar OD, McAlister A. Preventing the onset of smoking in Norwegian adolescents: the Oslo youth study. *Prev Med* 1984; **13**: 256–75.

12. Reid DJ. Prevention of smoking among schoolchildren: recommendations for policy development. *Health Educ J* 1985; **44**: 3–12.
13. Newman R, Smith C, Nutbeam D. Teachers' views of the 'Smoking and Me' project. *Health Educ J* 1991; **50**: 107–10.
14. Glynn T. Essential elements of school-based smoking prevention programs: research results. *J Sch Health* 1989; **59**: 181–8.
15. Cullen J. How to help the world stop smoking: interventions we should make. In: Durston, Jamrozik, Daube (eds). *The global war—Proc 7th world conference on tobacco and health*. Perth, WA: Department of Health 1990.
16. Corlette S, Eaton F. *Outcome evaluation of the Peer-Assisted Learning(PAL) smoking prevention program*. Ottawa: Health and Welfare Canada project report 1986.
17. Ross JG. Effectiveness of a health education curriculum for secondary school students—United States, 1986–89. *Centers for Disease Control Morbidity and Mortality Weekly Report* 1991; **40**: 113–6.
18. Murray DM et al. Five and six year follow up results from four seventh grade smoking prevention strategies. *J Behav Med* 1989; **12**: 207–18.
19. US Department of Health and Human Services (A). *Reducing the health consequences of smoking: 25 years of progress*. A report of the Surgeon General. DHHS Pub No (CDC) 89-8411, pre-publication version, January 1989; 591.
20. Best JA, Thompson SJ, Santi SM, Smith EA, Brown KS. Preventing cigarette smoking among schoolchildren. *Ann Rev Public Health* 1988; **9**: 161–201.
21. Bellew W, Wayne D. Prevention of smoking among schoolchildren: review of research and recommended actions. *Health Educ J* 1991; **50**: 3–8.
22. Aaro LE et al. Smoking among Norwegian schoolchildren 1975–80: the effect of anti-smoking campaigns. *Scand J Psychol* 1983; **24**: 277–83.
23. Newman R, Nutbeam D. Teachers' views of the Family Smoking Education Project. *Health Educ J* 1989; **48**(1): 9–13.
24. Charlton A. Evaluation of a family linked smoking programme in primary schools. *Health Educ J* 1986; **45**(3): 140–4.
25. Charlton A. Evaluation of a family-linked smoking programme in primary schools. *Health Educ J* 1986; **45**(3): 140–4.
26. Murray M et al. The effectiveness of the Health Education Council's 'My Body' school health education project. *Health Educ J* 1982; **41**: 126–30.
27. Goddard E. *Smoking among secondary school children in England in 1988*. OPCS for the Department of Health. London: HMSO 1989.
28. US Department of Health and Human Services (B). *Reducing the health consequences of smoking: 25 years of progress*. A report of the Surgeon General. DHHS Pub No (CDC) 89-8411, pre-publication version, January 1989; 269, 303.
29. Chapman S. Stop-smoking clinics: a case for their abandonment. *Lancet* 1985; **i**: 918–20.
30. Males M. Youth behaviour: subcultural effect or mirror of adult behaviour? *J Sch Health* 1990; **60**: 505–8.
31. Doll R. Conversation with Sir Richard Doll. *Br J Addict* 1991; **86**: 365–77.
32. Lewit EM, Coate D, Grossman M. The effects of government regulations on teenage smoking. *J Law Econ* 1981; **14**: 545–69.

33. Reid DJ, Smith N. What is the single most important intervention for the prevention of smoking-related disease? In: Durston, Jamrozik, Daube (eds). *The global war—Proc 7th world conference on tobacco and health*. Perth, WA: Department of Health 1990.
34. Adriaanse H, van Reik J. Teachers' smoking worldwide: a review of 19 countries (1966–83). *Int Q Community Health Educ* 1986; **7**: 3–17.
35. Rimpela M, Rimpela A, Kannas L. *Smoking*. Helsinki: National Board of Health Original Reports (4) 1983.
36. Brown KS, Santi S, Best JA. *The school and smoking prevention: the role of the school environment*. Paper presented at 6th International Conference on Smoking and Health, Tokyo, Japan 1987.
37. Charlton A. So what is your school's smoking policy? *Educ Health* 1985; **3**: 7–113.
38. Myers KA. An overview of school smoking policies in England and Wales. *Health Educ J* 1989; **48**(3): 110–2.
39. Pentz M et al. The power of policy: the relationship of smoking policy to adolescent smoking. *Am J Public Health* 1989; **79**: 857–62.
40. Fielding JE. Smoking control at the workplace. *Ann Rev Public Health* 1991; **12**: 209–34.
41. Flay BR, Sobel JL. *The role of the mass media in preventing adolescent substance misuse*. Health Behavior Research Institute, University of Southern California, 1985 Zonal Avenue, Los Angeles, California. 1985.
42. Glynn T. *US campaigns to reduce and prevent tobacco use among youth: review and recommendations*. Paper presented at DHSS/HEA Seminar on Mass Media Strategies to Reduce Tobacco Use Among Teenagers. Bristol, United Kingdom. Available from the HEA, London 1987.
43. Health Education Authority. *MORI teenage tracking study 3*. Report to the HEA 1991.
44. Worden JK et al. Development of a smoking prevention mass media program using diagnostic and formative research. *Prev Med* 1988; **17**: 531–58.
45. Bauman KE et al. The influence of three mass media campaigns on variables related to adolescent cigarette smoking: results of a field experiment. *Am J Public Health* 1991; **81**: 597–604.
46. Nutbeam D, Aaro LR. Smoking and pupil attitudes towards school: the implications for health education with young people. Results for the WHO study of health behaviour among school children. *Health Educ Res* 1991; **6**(4): 415–21.
47. Van Teijlingen ER, Friend JAR. Smoking habits of Grampian schoolchildren and an evaluation of the Grampian Smokebusters Campaign. *Health Educ Res*. In Press.
48. Health Promotion Authority for Wales. *Welsh youth health survey 1986: protocol and questionnaire*. Heartbeat Wales Technical Report No. 5. Cardiff: Health Promotion Authority for Wales 1986.
49. Gillies P, Elwood JM, Pearson JCG, Cust G. An adolescent smoking survey in Trent and its contribution to health promotion. *Health Educ J* 1987; **46**: 19–22.
50. Health Promotion Authority for Wales. *Implementation of non-smoking policies in hospitals in Wales 1987–89*. Heartbeat Wales Briefing Report No. 2. Cardiff: Health Promotion Authority for Wales 1991.
51. Goddard E. *Why children start smoking*. OPCS for the Department of

Health. London: HMSO 1990.

52. Catford J, Woolaway M, Batten L, Nutbeam D. Quitting for life—the role of health authorities in smoking cessation. *Health Educ J* 1985; **44**(1): 31–5.

53. Amos A, Robertson G, Hillhouse A. Tobacco advertising and children: widespread breaches of the voluntary agreement. *Health Educ Res* 1987; **2**(3): 207–14.

54. *Tobacco price and the smoking epidemic: smoke-free Europe.* World Health Organisation, 1988.

55. Smith C. Smoking among young people: some recent developments in Wales. *Health Educ J* 1991; **50**(1): 8–11.

56. Health Education Authority. *MORI teenage tracking study 3.* London: Health Education Authority 1991.

57. Naidoo J, Platts C. Smoking prevention in Bristol: getting maximum results using minimum resources. *Health Educ J* 1985; **44**: 39–42.

58. Altman DG *et al.* Reducing the illegal sale of cigarettes to minors. *J Am Med Assoc* 1989; **261**: 80–3.

59. Health Education Authority. Correspondence between the Chairman of the Health Education Council and the Tobacco Advisory Council. 1991.

60. Cragg, Ross, Dawson Research Partnership. *Health warnings on cigarette and tobacco packets: report on research to inform European standardisation.* December 1990. London: Health Education Authority.

61. *Ending an epidemic.* Action on Smoking and Health 1991.

62. Catford JC. Health targets: time to put the NHS back on course. *Br Med J* 1991; **302**: 980–1.

63. Collishaw N. Trends in Canadian tobacco consumption 1980–87. *Chronic Diseases in Canada* 1988; **9**: 105–7.

64. California Department of Health Services. *Tobacco use in California 1990.* A preliminary report documenting the decline of tobacco use. University of San Diego 1991.

65. New Zealand Toxic Substances Board. *Health or tobacco—an end to tobacco advertising and promotion.* Wellington, New Zealand: Department of Health 1989.

60. House of Commons Written Answers, 11 March 1991; Col 378.

61. Joossens L, Raw M. Tobacco and the European Common Agricultural Policy. *Br J Addict* 1991; **86**: 1191–202.

62. Royal College of Physicians. *Smoking and health.* London: Royal College of Physicians 1962.

63. *The case against tobacco advertising.* Coronary Prevention Group, 1991.

64. *Eurobarometer report for the Economic Community.* October 1991.

65. Tobacco Advisory Council. *The case for tobacco advertising.* London Advisory Council 1985.

66. Aitken PP. *From the bill-board to the playground.* CRC 1991.

67. Aitken PP, Leathar DS, O'Hagan FJ. Children's perceptions of advertisements for cigarettes. *Soc Sci Med* 1985; **21**: 785–97.

68. Charlton A. Children's advertisement awareness related to their views on smoking. *Health Educ J* 1986; **45**: 75–8.

69. Alexander HM *et al.* Cigarette smoking and drug use in school children. IV. Factors associated with changes in smoking behaviour. *Int J Epidemiol* 1983; **12**: 59–66.

70. Potts H, Gillies PA, Herbert M. Adolescent smoking and opinion of

cigarette advertisements. *Health Educ Res* 1986; **1**: 195–201.
71. Nelson EM, Charlton A. Children and advertising: does the voluntary agreement work? *Health Educ J* 1991; **50**: issue 1.
72. Pierce JP *et al.* Does tobacco advertising target young people to start smoking? *J Am Med Assoc* 1991; **226**: 3154–8.
73. Piepe A, Charlton P, Morey J, White C, Yerrell P. Smoke opera? *Health Educ J* 1986; **45**: 199–203.
74. Ledwith F. Does tobacco sport sponsorship on television act as advertising to children? *Health Educ J* 1984; **43**: 85–8.
75. Magnus P. Superman and the Marlboro woman: the lungs of Lois Lane. *N Y State J Med* 1985; **85**(7): 342–3.
76. The sponsors' racing formula. *Newsweek* 21 March 1983.
77. Media Register, 1990.
78. House of Commons Written Answers, 11 March 1991.
79. Dunlop M, McBride G, Raw M, Walker A. Worldwide moves against tobacco promotion. *Br Med J* 1990; **301**: 458–60.
80. Laugesen M, Meads C. Tobacco advertising restrictions, price, income and tobacco consumption in OECD countries, 1960–86. *Br J Addict* 1991; **86**: 1343–54.
81. Bjartveit K. *Fifteen years of comprehensive legislation: results and conclusions.* Proceedings of the 7th World Conference on Tobacco and Health. Perth 1990.
82. *Tobacco advertising bans work!* Action on Smoking and Health, 1991.
83. Dickson N. BBC Radio 4, 10 January 1992.